ARE YOU
DRIVEN 2 WIN?

A Roadmap for Young People to Succeed in Life

An Inspirational Activity Workbook

WRITTEN BY
RAMONA S. JONES

BOOK ILLUSTRATIONS BY
JOAQUIN JUNCO JR.

AUTHOR PHOTO BY
TRE ARNOLD

authorHOUSE®

AuthorHouse™
1663 Liberty Drive
Bloomington, IN 47403
www.authorhouse.com
Phone: 1 (800) 839-8640

Published by AuthorHouse   10/19/2017

ISBN: 978-1-5462-0901-0 (sc)
ISBN: 978-1-5462-0900-3 (e)

Print information available on the last page.

Any people depicted in stock imagery provided by Thinkstock are models, and such images are being used for illustrative purposes only. Certain stock imagery © Thinkstock.

This book is printed on acid-free paper.

I want, first of all, to say I am thankful for the DREAMbuilders vision I was given decades ago. Without vision, there would be no manifestation. I am thankful for my assignment to inspire, motivate, and encourage all to pursue their dreams with a vengeance. See it. Believe it. Speak it. Be it. Receive it. You hold the keys to manifest the destiny for which you were born in the first place.

To my daughters, Rachelle and Rayna - DREAM your dreams and do not give up. Don't let Life stamp out your dreams. Live your life and stare fear in the face. Get a fire in you. Climb your mountains, challenge your giants, and seize your greatness! Create a soft place to land when you brave the storms. Be good to yourselves by loving your essence and the people assigned to you. I love you. I shine when you shine. DREAMbuilders exists and was made for you. Be Driven 2 Win. Be D2W. You have a prepared path for your life. You are designed and destined to win.

TABLE OF CONTENTS

APPENDICES

FOREWORD

Can young people make the right decisions when it really counts? All too often the age of information has made decision-making even more complicated. Information is everywhere. Everything is at your fingertips. With this accessibility come responsibility and the ability to choose what is good information versus information that can destroy a future. I have known Mrs. Ramona Jones for over 30 years and this is not just work for her, but a passion to assist young people to be prepared for life. 'Are YOU Driven 2 Win? A Roadmap for Young People to Succeed' book is an answer to what her mission in life has been which is to uplift and empower every young person in America.

In today's society young people are susceptible to many invisible and visible threats to their success. There are young people with a mind to accomplish great things and they are exhausting all opportunities to prepare themselves to win in every facet of life, but threats are staring them in the face challenging them to settle for less and die with their dreams inside themselves. It really does not matter what community they come from. From the wealthiest to the most impoverished families, threats are obstacles to the strong will and perseverance it takes to make any dream a reality. Threats can be as intense as incarceration, recidivism, teenage pregnancy, trafficking, promiscuity, depression, sickness, or merely distractions and pitfalls pushing you off course to your future. This is why I am so highly impressed with how Mrs. Ramona Jones has conceptualized the winning mindset as being 'Driven 2 Win or D2W.' What better way for young people to visualize themselves staring fear and failure in the face and being brave enough to "drive" into their future by making the right decisions and taking action.

Mrs. Ramona Jones has ingeniously used the driving analogy to help young people visualize where they are headed by helping them to focus on responsible decision-making centered on values, vision, and goals while overcoming problems and obstacles. Every youth in America should read this book and prepare themselves to confidently answer the questions to begin finding their path, understanding their motivations, and answering the important questions that will shape their careers and future. *What do I want to do with my life? What kind of person do I want to be? Where am I headed? What roads will I choose?* These questions start the process of navigating life and making decisions that prepare the roads to a promising future. As a workforce development specialist with over 30 years of experience, I can honestly say that this work is one of the most effective, comprehensive personal development books available on the market to inspire young people to use their God-given talents, build a vision and plan, and take courage to navigate their lives forward. This book is a must-have for all young people because they must be aware of the frailty of life and how humbling it is to one day look up and ask yourself: *"How did I get here?"*

I strongly recommend this book as a top priority for any parent who is seeking a strong, motivating influence and message to keep their young person centered and focused on accomplishing their dreams and goals. I also recommend this valued resource to schools, youth ministries, and any youth-serving agency with the mission to prepare the next generation of leaders who are competent visionaries prepared to "win" in their own lives as well as impact their generation for greater tomorrows.

John F. Weber
Former Employment Program Manager
Employment Development Department in Silicon Valley/San Jose, CA

PREFACE

'Are You Driven 2 Win: A Roadmap for Young People to Succeed in Life' book was written to teach young people the secrets of how to be strong, brave, and bold to navigate through Life's opportunities and challenges. In this book, you will hear the voice of a mentor. This is who I am. My role is to encourage and inspire you to push forward on your personal journey. One thing about life is that you don't have to do it alone. There is always someone to learn from. There is always someone ahead of you guiding and showing the way forward. Other people's life experiences, if evaluated and studied, contain a gold mine of mentoring examples that could really help you in making quality decisions about your own life.

If you are wise, you will listen and learn. If you are not, you will not think twice about the advice, but will later in life bump up against challenges and problems that you could have been avoided. I have experienced so many things in life and now have perspective to give you some hard-earned advice. I hope you will be one of those wise students.

This is not an Algebra or Science class. However, it is a class in Life. There will be lectures. There will be a test. It will not be my test, but it will be the continual tests that Life will give you whenever it is ready for you to take it. Don't be surprised. There will be surprise quizzes too. You will not always have the opportunity to study. You must always prepare yourself. One of my dear friends says, "If you stay ready, you won't have to get ready." This is a good lesson to learn now.

Just maybe, I might say something your parents and guardians have been saying for years, but you haven't listened. Be wise and listen. Figure out the purpose of the words and how you can use them to manage your life and win. Think of this book as your playbook to win in the game of life. Extending the driving analogy, this is a roadmap for you to succeed in life. The D2W Roadmap. I know you are ready to jump in the car and 'drive your life forward.' Get the roadmap first. Study what others have done. Get some perspective. You need mentors in your life to come and share their experiences and give you some advice.

It is not about telling you what to do, but about guiding you to make the best decisions. We want you to win. We want you to experience a great life.

Let me introduce you to the Driven 2 Win characters. Michael, Greg, and Antonio are the D2W guys. Janice, Eliza, and Melanie are the D2W ladies. They are your peer mentors. They will teach you a lot about life because they are going through what you are going through or a similar situation you may encounter at some point. They will show you the ropes. Read their stories. Read about their successes and failures. Their scenarios will portray what is being taught in each chapter or lesson. Each one of them has a dream, a desire to live their best life, and win.

DRIVEN 2 WIN CHARACTERS

J A N I C E

I spend most of my free time practicing ballet. I don't have a lot of time to hang out with friends. Melanie and I have been best friends in ballet since we were age 5. My family does not have a lot of extra money, but I babysit to pay for my lessons. I like to act and sing, but ballet is my #1 passion.

I am Driven 2 Win.

I am D2W.

M I C H A E L

This year I am not letting anything stop me. I will try out for the Varsity football team. My desire is to get a full-ride scholarship to play in college and maybe the pros. I need some help keeping my grades up and also not being distracted by my girlfriend Melanie. My best friend Greg is always giving me advice on how to deal with the ladies.

I am Driven 2 Win.

I am D2W.

M E L A N I E

My friends are really important to me. My family owns a successful business and every year we go on exotic vacations and I get to bring a few friends. I am doing well in school, but I am bored. I am tired of ballet and my best friend Janice will not understand if I quit. I love going to formal dances and shopping at the mall with friends. My dad gives me a lot of money and I spend it on looking good for my boyfriend Michael.

I am Driven 2 Win.

I am D2W.

A N T O N I O

I am not a sports junkie like most guys, but I am a whiz at chess. I have had a crush on Eliza since middle school. She is one year older than me and doesn't know I exist. I am smart, plan to go to college, and have big goals to help my family. I struggle with my weight, but I do not let it get me down.

I am Driven 2 Win.

I am D2W.

G R E G

I lift weights. It is important for me to look good.
My best friend is Michael and he is always trying to get me
to play football. Right now, I am on the basketball team,
but not for long. My main desire is to save up for a car and
make some money. I work at Bucky Burgers, but
I need to find a way to get some real money.
I am Driven 2 Win.
I am D2W.

E L I Z A

I have big plans for my life. I want to travel around the world and
have a successful career. I am not sure what I want to do yet, but
my mentor is helping me explore careers. I am opinionated and
I like to write. I am not scared to speak in public.
I have a younger sister that looks up to me. I have to do well.
I will be the first one to finish college in my family.
I am excited about my life.
I am Driven 2 Win.
I am D2W.

In this book, there are seven introductory chapters to get you thinking about your life. The next section of the book provides 20 powerful chapters organized in three sections introducing the D2W Life Management System. Each chapter and lesson has three unique items. There are D2W character scenarios providing examples of how the D2W characters demonstrate the concepts shared. There is a D2W Stoplight where I summarize the life concepts provided. There is a corresponding activity called 'D2W: It's Your Turn' for you to apply the concepts to your life. The final chapter describes how all these concepts and lessons work together to create your own personal D2W Roadmap. You will learn how to visually 'put your life on the road' by using the D2W Life Management System.

For those that are not avid readers, you do not have to be. Learn the D2W Life Management System. Read one chapter every day. Do the corresponding activity in the workbook. You will be done in 30 days. For those avid readers, you might be done with this book in a week. Do not read it like other books. Do not read to get through the text. Take your time and ponder what is being said. Read it, pick it up, put it down, think about it, and pick it up again. This is not a book you read once and toss to the side. I want you to look inside yourself. You are studying yourself. You are the subject. How different is that? This is your training. Trust the training will prepare you to be ready for the opportunities and challenges that will come your way. Life is unpredictable at times. Life is not perfect. You have to prepare yourself to win in life. This is where it starts. Get ready to win. **Be Driven 2 Win. Be D2W.**

Chapter 1: Are You Driven to Win?

Are You DRIVEN 2 WIN? I like to say, 'Are you D2W?' **What does it mean to be Driven 2 Win or D2W?** It means you are a winner on the inside first and eventually outside. You think like a winner. You act like a winner. You perform like a winner. *Doesn't everyone want to win in life?* If you are playing basketball or football, don't you want your team to win? When you are at an awards banquet, don't you want them to call your name so you can walk on stage and get the trophy, the medal, or the prize money? Winners get the trophies. Winners get the prizes. **Life is competitive. What's the point of playing the game, if you are not rewarded for your effort?** I know there is value in just playing the game and being a part of the experience, but competition prepares you for life.

Why are you Driven 2 Win? Why are you D2W? This is just like asking: What motivates you? What moves you to win or what makes you get up and do your best work? Sometimes this question is easy to answer and sometimes it is not. What motivates you today can change as you get older. It might have been important for you to get good grades when you were in elementary and middle school to make your parents proud and bring home a report card full of A's and B's. What about now? When you are age 18 and considered an adult on your college campus, will you still be motivated to get good grades because of your parents? Probably not. At least that should not be the only motivator. What will be your motivation then? I cannot answer that for you. That question belongs to you. Your motivation will mature as you mature. What motivates you today to make the necessary effort toward a specific goal may not be enough to motivate you tomorrow.

If you asked me when I was in high school what motivated me to do well in school and get good grades, it would have probably been that I wanted to make my mother and dad proud of me. I wanted my family to see me as someone who was smart and capable. This motivation is still true even though I am an adult now. Most people are motivated to do well in life because they want someone they love to be proud of them. What others think and believe about you is usually a strong motivator. It is not the only motivator and should not be. Back in the day, it was really important to young people that their teachers thought highly of them, so they brought apples or gifts to school and presented them to their favorite teachers. You ever heard of these stories? Ask your parents. Well maybe I did not ever do that, but I remember wanting very much to be liked by my teachers and wanting their affection and approval as one of the best and brightest in the classroom. These motivations are not as apparent in today's classrooms; however, some students really are motivated to be the prize students in class.

Are you motivated to be the smartest or brightest in your class? Some students are competitive in school and are really motivated to be the best in Algebra class or get the highest score on the test. You might be motivated to be the valedictorian of your school. You might desire to go to the most prestigious universities. You know anyone like this? What is happening in these instances is that high value is being placed on academic performance. Is this right? Is this wrong? It is not a right or wrong issue. It simply is. It is a part of a person's value system. It gives people meaning. Is this the only motivation? NO.

Do you know what motivates you? What is driving you? If you say you are 'Driven to Win,' what does that look like? We are talking about your reason to do well in life. What is so important to you that nobody has to scream in your ear over and over to do it? Is it academics? Is it your abilities at sports? What about how well you sing or write or how well you dress? Does that mean you are focused on accomplishing your goals? If you are trying out for a play, does that mean you want the lead role? If you are 'Driven to Win,' does that mean you are the first one at football practice, and you are lifting weights before all the other players? What about making an appointment with your career counselor so you can find all the college scholarships you can apply for? To me, these are examples of people demonstrating they are motivated. They are 'Driven to Win.' They are focused. They are putting forth their best efforts. They want something for themselves and willing to go get it. Whatever it is, their motivation is linked to their value system.

Let's agree that it is important to determine the source of your motivation. Your motivation can be positive, and it also can be negative. For example, if you are motivated to get into college because it would make you feel proud of your accomplishments that you were the first one in your family to become a college graduate, then I would say that is very positive. However, if the root of your motivation was to outdo your friends, or prove to someone you loved who always said that you would not amount to anything, that could be seen as negative. There are people who tell themselves, "When I get older I will show them," and this becomes the source of their motivation. Being led by healthy thinking is always the better route in the short and long run. **One thing is clear that the most powerful motivation is going to stem from what you want to prove and do for yourself.** It is okay to include others as the initial source of your motivation, but satisfying them may not be enough in the long run, and you must eventually mature into caring enough for yourself to make something out of your life.

When I was in high school, I participated in speech competition. This extracurricular school event would be a defining area of my self-confidence the same way if you were the top basketball player on a winning team at your school. Speech competition was my life. It was the one area that I was truly celebrated. I received dozens of trophies, qualified and did extremely well at state and national championships. Every time I came home from a tournament, my mother would say, "Where's my trophy?" She was very proud of me. After six years of competition, these trophies and medals were displayed on several bookcases in our family living room as a place of honor. She would tell her co-workers. My whole family was aware of my high school and college success.

Once I tasted success and recognition, I made sure I put in the effort to be one of the best. I was extremely motivated to do well and be competitive. I wanted to make myself proud, along with my mother and my speech coach. For four years, my speech coach, Clifford Roach from El Camino High School in Oceanside, California, was instrumental in my personal success. Of all my teachers, he was the one person that I had to impress. When I practiced my speeches in front of him, I was always so nervous. I could see on his face when he was touched by my dramatic scenes. I could sense his pride when I came back with 'Best Speaker' or first place trophies from the tournament. When I was a senior in high school, I was the speech president. I was motivated to keep our team a winning school. It was so important to my life that when I was a senior, I qualified for the National Speech Championship in

Cincinnati, Ohio, but the competition fell on the same day of my senior graduation. Instead of attending my own graduation and walking with my classmates, I chose to leave and compete in the event of my life.

Was it worth it? I placed in the semi-finals after competing with hundreds of students throughout the United States. Thousands had competed, and I was proud of my accomplishments. Yes, it was worth it. The trophies and medals are gone now after all these years, but the effort and dedication to obtain them live on through the memories and experiences lived. What I have described for you was the source of my motivation while I was in high school and college. However, my motivation has changed and developed beyond this. It would be ridiculous to still be motivated to impress my speech coach. I have moved beyond that initial motivation, and now I am motivated by other things and reasons. I was motivated to finish my college degrees because I wanted to earn more money. I also wanted to feel proud of my academic accomplishments, probably in part because my mother had gone to college, and like her, I expected to attain a college degree.

No doubt some of you might have sisters and brothers who finished college and you feel like you have to measure up. Let's be honest. Whether that is a good reason or not, many people are motivated to do things because they do not want to be outdone by others or they want to look good to themselves and others. If these motivations are similar to yours, I say be honest and use them to your advantage. Just make sure you challenge yourself to grow past being motivated for superficial reasons and move toward more positive, mentally healthy reasons.

Let me give you an example of a negative motivator. I knew one young middle school kid who had a lot of problems. He would always be the class clown and do something "silly." He would tease and bother other students until a fight was started, and then he would be suspended from school. He would continually be punished by his dad for not coming into the house before it got dark or he would be put on restriction because he was caught playing in an area that his dad said was too dangerous. Whatever he was told not to do, he found himself doing and getting into trouble. I shared that story with you because his dad would always say,

"You are going to do the wrong thing, aren't you? I can expect you to act up at the school field trip and your teacher will have to call me, right?" His motivation became to prove his dad wrong. Sometimes he did and sometimes he failed. This is an example of using a negative motivator. It may work for a while, but eventually, you have to recognize the source of your reason or your "why" for performing well and mature beyond negative motivators to healthy reasons for personal growth and achievement.

We are not always motivated to do our best. Sometimes we are not ready to drive forward. Our actions take us places where we really do not want to be, but we drive our lives there anyway. I'll give you a few examples. What if football is your life and you lose the ball to the opposing team, and this error allows them to win the championship game? Instead of recovering emotionally from this situation, you withdraw and become depressed, drop out of football, stop being motivated to keep your grades up, and eventually quit school. Now that would really be a depressing situation. I made it up, but negative situations happen, and we become 'Driven to Lose.' We go through problems, we get upset at life, ourselves, or even others, and we start thinking and acting in ways that make us go backward.

Since we are identifying what motivates or drives us, what could possibly cause us to go backward? Sometimes when we have done something wrong we feel guilty. *"I will not try out for the play because I don't deserve to get a part anyway."* Why would you feel that way when you love theater? Maybe you are motivated to make yourself suffer? Maybe you are angry at your parents. *"It sure would hurt my parents if I failed at school. I am angry at them."* To straighten our lives out, we have to dig deep and get to the root of our motivations. Whatever the case, you can understand that motivation is powerful and it needs to be rooted from a healthy, positive place to bring lasting results in your life.

Michael could not wait until football season started. He was charged up every time he thought about the conversation he had with his football coach last semester. Was he really good enough to make it to the pros? Everyone kept saying he could really go all the way if he continued to put the effort in. This was his chance to prove to his family that he was focused and motivated to make this happen for himself. His first step was to make the varsity football team at his high school. He could see the smile on his dad's face once he accomplished that goal. His brothers were good, but Michael was great. He was determined and ready to go all the way with his dream.

This D2W example involves competitive sports. However, there are areas to win in besides sports. Any activity you are involved in will require you to be motivated to do your best and has the ability to shape your mindset to be one of a winner.

Eliza did not care what her cousins said. Her family did not have the money, but once her counselor talked about the overseas trip to Europe, she could not stop thinking about it. Her family was always consumed with financial problems, and they never went on vacations. She thought it would be great to travel to another country, meet other people, and maybe she could go to school or get a job in Europe. This was her chance to see the world and think bigger than any person she knew in her family. The trip would cost $1,500, but there had to be a way to make money. It was her dream to travel the world and see other cultures. This was a big challenge, but she was motivated to find some answers.

These D2W scenarios are examples of young people that are D2W or Driven 2 Win. They want something. That means they do not have it right now. They are motivated to work hard for it, and they have decided the "prize" is worth the effort. *Michael – "I really want to have a football career. I am motivated to prove to my parents I can do it."* Eliza – *"I really want to travel. I am motivated to experience new things and opportunities."* What would you love to create for your life? Are you motivated and are you willing to work hard for it?

D2W Stop Sign Alert

It is important to focus your attention on what you want to accomplish in life. Make a quality decision and figure out why your goals are valuable to you. If your motivation is strong and stems from a positive, healthy mindset, then as you accomplish your goals, you will grow as a person.

D2W Assignment: It's Your Turn

Answer the questions below.

I really want to _____   I am motivated because _____

I really want to _____   I am motivated because _____

I really want to _____   I am motivated because _____

Chapter 2: Driving in the Winning Lane

Nobody dreams of being in last place. Everyone wants to be a winner. Of course, my definition of winning in life might be different than yours. There is not always an easy definition of winning. Winning can be elusive or hard to figure out sometimes. I cannot define what winning is for you. **Everyone must define what winning is for themselves**. Life does not give out gold medals for everything you are involved in. It is easy to declare the winner in a baseball game, but how do you decide who the winner is in life? Who is keeping score? What is winning? Is it how much money you have? Is it a successful career? What about good grades? Maybe it is being the prettiest girl or the best dressed? To say that these areas are not what most people consider success is to be a little naïve, but we all know these areas are a few examples of success, though not the only measurements of success. One day everyone is congratulating you for winning the big basketball game and then the next game you are ducking everybody's stare because you missed all your jump shots. There is a quote by Vince Lombardi that goes, *"Winning isn't everything, it's the only thing."* Do you believe that? You have known people or know people who must win at everything or their world is crushed. This is a very hard place to be because it is difficult to win at everything. At some point, failure or failed experiences will come. Life challenges you to look at who you are on the inside while you win or lose on the outside.

Everyone has the opportunity to win. What we have to remember is that the only one we are ultimately competing with is ourselves. That means your own personal success is measured on a scale that aligns with what you value or what you consider is important. You alone are the final judge to say you are proud of yourself. You know yourself. You know when you put real effort into whatever you do. When you work hard, and you challenge your own mediocrity, you can be proud of yourself regardless of the outcome. You might not win in everyone else's book, but you definitely should win in your own book. If there is someone better than you (and there will be, at times), give them their props, but do not discount your own.

It is safe to say that you feel like a winner at times and sometimes you might feel like a loser. Do not rely on or expect to feel successful or like a winner every moment of the day. We do not always FEEL like a winner. Feelings are flimsy. Feelings cannot be depended on. Feelings are based on your circumstances. They cannot support your faith in who you are and what you will become. If I had to depend on how I felt to move me toward doing what it takes to succeed, I would not have finished my college degrees, built relationships, established a business, or even finished this book. Real success cannot survive being dependent on how you feel, anyway. Sometimes you feel like life is great, and everything is working. Other times you are overwhelmed with problems that you feel depressed. It's not about your feelings; it is about your faith. Have faith in your purpose and calling. Move past FEELINGS; move into FAITH. What do you believe? What do you believe about who you are and what you can achieve? Stand on that and that alone. Make it your mission to use up all your potential while you are breathing and keep challenging your mediocrity. Move past the status quo.

That's when life gets magical. That is what you can be proud of. Be proud of your individual efforts that get you to your next level of greatness. Those are your trophies.

Who are you competing against? Who are your competitors? **We should never make others the source of our ultimate comparison. We compete with our own potential and desire.** It is never someone else because that is sure failure and a cheapening of our self-worth. Why is this so, you may ask? Well, what if you determined that winning in life is based on whether you do better than your sister in school. What if your sister was in special education and the level of her capabilities and performance was drastically different than yours. She brings home a grade of C on her math test, and you bring home a grade of B on your test. You believe you have done better than her. This comparison is biased and wrong. Your sister is in special education and also younger than you. Your academic and comprehension level is vastly different. It would be unfair to consider yourself as equals. In the same sense, if your sister was not in special education and, instead of her intelligence, you considered her more successful than you because she had an incredible singing voice and wanted to be a famous singer one day. It would also be wrong for you to compare yourself to her. What am I saying? **You have your own lane. You win in your lane, not somebody else's.** Does that make sense? Your task is to figure out your lane by discovering your talents and interests and pursue them with all that you've got.

The main thing when you are transitioning or navigating from young adult to adulthood is to identify what you want out of life and go after it. If it is meaningful to you, then you will take a lot of pride at what you do. Not everybody thinks the same things are important. For example, it may be life and death for you to get all A's on your report card, but another student may not hold themselves to those standards. Who is right or wrong? It is not about being right or wrong. Who is a winner or a loser? It really is not about that either.

You determine what is important for your life. You will declare yourself a winner according to what you value. The really sad thing is that sometimes we bury ourselves in guilt because we have unfair expectations and rules we try to live by. For example, what if you believed you were a failure if you did not get the lead part in the play? You might say that is ridiculous. Well, if all your life you auditioned and got lead parts and everyone in your family made a big fuss about how well you performed in theater, then you could reasonably hold yourself to that high standard and always expect to get the lead parts. If you do not measure up to your expectation and do not get the lead part, would you fall apart and consider you failed? **When you define and measure your personal success on an unfair scale, then you fall into the trap of judging yourself as a loser or failure.**

I'll give you another example. What if you needed a grade of B on your upcoming History exam to pull your 3.2 GPA to a 3.5 GPA and get into the same college with your best friend? Even though you studied for weeks, you still got a grade of C. You finished with a 3.2 GPA and did not get into the college you wanted. Would you judge yourself as a loser or failure based on this experience?

One last scenario. What if your dream was like the D2W character Michael and you put all your dreams into a football scholarship? All throughout high school, your parents, coaches, friends, and teachers kept saying how good you were at football. They continually told you that you were good enough to make it all the way to the NFL. You believed it. You wanted it for yourself, but it did not happen for you. **Are you a loser? Are you a winner?** This might not be your story, but believe me, there are people in the world still affected today by what did or did not happen for them. It doesn't have to be football. It could be anything that you really desired for yourself and put all of your might into trying to get it. **What do you do now?**

Well, the first thing for us to remember is to not limit success to what is happening to us only externally, but expand our definition to also include what is happening inside of us. **Success is measured not only by what we accomplish, but also by how we have developed on the inside.** This is one way to explain how failed experiences crush some people's initiative to keep trying while others bounce back from it. Everyone succeeds, and everyone fails. *"Success is to be measured not so much by the position that one has reached in life as by the obstacles which he has overcome while trying to succeed." (Booker T. Washington)* It comes down to what you believe about yourself on the inside.

So, what is driving in the winning lane? 'Driving in the winning lane' means you are aware of your goals, you know the areas that you need to strengthen, and you are motivated and committed to keep working and striving toward better decisions and performance. That's it. What else can you ask of yourself? *"The dictionary is the only place that success comes before work. Hard work is the price we must pay for success. I think you can accomplish anything if you're willing to pay the price." (Vince Lombardi)* When it comes down to winning or succeeding in life, it really is about the hard work and effort you put toward fulfilling your goals. It is not about what everyone else is doing or even what they want you to do. Your life should be about working toward the things that are important to you, accomplishing things that you can be proud of, and living with your decisions. If you can do that, you definitely will be driving in the winning lane.

D2W Character Scenario

Janice and Melanie were best friends ever since elementary school. They met in ballet class and their families were inseparable. Now that they were in high school they were not hanging out like they used to. Janice was always talking about practicing for a new ballet recital and Melanie was always hanging out with her new boyfriend, Michael. Melanie had no interest in ballet now, but Janice was more passionate than ever. Ballet was her life and if she had her way she would be a professional dancer. Ballet was her passion.

D2W Stop Sign Alert

Winning in life is personal. Build your strengths and skills so you can be successful in your activities. When you give your best effort, you win. Life is competitive. Work hard to get your physical trophies, but your personal satisfaction is your #1 trophy.

Answer the questions below.

What was the last thing you achieved? _____

What efforts did you do to achieve success? _____

How were you recognized, rewarded, or acknowledged? _____

Are you proud of your accomplishments? _____

What are you working on now to achieve your next win? _____

Chapter 3: Are You Ready to Drive? Can You Pass the Test of Maturity?

Life is about tests. I know you are excited to get the keys to your own car and drive one day. You need to understand that, before you can do that, you have to pass your driving test. Driving is a privilege, and most young people feel like this opportunity separates them from being a kid and asupern adult. This is an exciting time. As a parent teaching my daughters to drive, which is no easy task, there is no greater fear for a parent. It took three attempts for my oldest daughter to pass her driving test. There were some turns she made while we were practicing that I thought we might not make it out alive. I must say getting your driver's license is a real achievement. Tests show what you know and they also show you what things you still need to know. Driving tests are not the only kinds of tests you will face. Whether it is making sure you come to a full stop or looking deliberately over your shoulder before you turn right, you will be faced with tests while driving a car and also as you journey toward maturity. Life brings several tests to you. *Why is this so, you may ask?* The tests Life brings your way come to determine if you are ready and mature enough for your next opportunities. If you do not pass the tests that Life gives you, you cannot advance to the next stages of your life.

What does it take to pass the tests that Life gives you? Smart decisions. When you make smart decisions, you build a bright future and drive your life forward. One way to determine if you are making the right decisions is if your life is working and you are being promoted to the next level of opportunities. Those opportunities might be greater leadership activities in your sports or school club, a job promotion, or your parents giving you more freedom and independence. Here are some decisions. You are turning in your school assignments on time. You are diligent at your part-time job and show up on time. You consistently make curfew, and you take care of the family car. You organize your calendar and keep up with all your appointments and commitments. These are examples of situations where you demonstrate your maturity and make sound decisions. If you continue on this path, you are showing that you are responsible and you are passing Life's tests of maturity. **Mature young adults understand they are responsible for their life.** This does not mean that you won't ever make a mistake or a wrong choice. **You understand your decisions create the life you will live.**

Just like a driving instructor tests you on making left turns, backing up, and parking a car, **Life presents situations that will test or challenge your maturity level.** If you cannot pass the maturity tests, you will have to repeat them until you do. Your life will be halted and delayed until you finally get it. There are four maturity areas that you must pass. By no means is this a complete listing, but many of the things you will face as a maturing young adult will fall into one of these categories. By meeting the requirements of these maturity areas, you demonstrate you are ready and can manage your life.

Four Maturity Tests

Maturity Test 1: Recognizing and meeting your responsibilities

Maturity Test 2: Building and maintaining healthy relationships

Maturity Test 3: Identifying and using resources

Maturity Test 4: Making and standing by your decisions

Maturity Test 1: *Recognizing and meeting your responsibilities*

Michael was so excited to have his driver's license finally. His parents let him borrow the family car to go out on the weekends. This weekend he planned to go to the movies with his friends. His parents' only request was to come home by his 11 pm curfew, bring the car back without dents, and with at least a half tank of gas. After the movies, Michael and his friends decided to go to Bucky Burgers. He was 30 minutes late driving home. He did not call, and he did not remember to fill up the gas tank. In the morning, his dad got dressed for work, put the car in reverse, and noticed the car was low on gas. Once again, Michael forgot to meet his responsibilities. As Michael grabbed his schoolbag, he heard his dad scream his name.

Maturity Test 1 is about recognizing and meeting your responsibilities.

This example shows the D2W character Michael not meeting his responsibilities.

What did Michael do in this scenario? He was late for his 11pm curfew and did not call. He also forgot to put gas in the tank before driving home. He was so focused on having a good time with his friends that he did not stop and take time to meet the responsibilities that he agreed to. There are all kinds of individual responsibilities

that can fit in this category. It might be taking out the trash without being told. It could be getting all your homework and your chores done before playing videos, or going outside. The tasks parents, teachers, coaches, or other authority figures give you are opportunities to demonstrate how mature you are. Your responsibilities are an example of an agreement. **"You do this, and then you can… (Fill in the blank)." If you meet curfew, you can go out with your friends. If you take out the trash, you will get an allowance.**

Get serious about passing your maturity tests and making the right decisions.

Can you pass Maturity Test 1: Recognizing and meeting your responsibilities?

Are you handling your responsibilities on your own without being reminded? Do you know what they are? Who is in the driver's seat? You are. Ask your parents how well you are passing this test. You're ready to be an adult, right? You want your license and a car so you can go where you want to go, right? Are you ready? Are you mature? **Maturity is not about age.** Your age is not necessarily a predictor if you are mature enough to handle life situations. It is about if you are ready to manage your life and make the best decisions. There are young people ages six and seven who can pass this maturity test better than teenagers. **The problem with being older and still not meeting your responsibilities is that others expect more of you.** If you are three years old, your parents probably do not expect you to take out the trash, but they may expect you to start to learn to put away your toys. At age ten, you probably cannot pass the high school equivalency test, but you should be able to recite your multiplicity facts or spell simple words. **The 'D' word comes to mind: Discipline, which means doing what it takes to get the job done even when you do not feel like it.** Make sure that, whatever age you are, you pass this test Life will continually give you.

D2W Assignment: It's Your Turn

Write down five responsibilities you have currently. Who is watching to see if you get them done correctly and timely? What is the impact if you do not get them done?

Responsibilities	Accountable Person	Impact
1. _____	_____	_____
2. _____	_____	_____
3. _____	_____	_____
4. _____	_____	_____
5. _____	_____	_____

Maturity Test 2: *Building and maintaining healthy relationships*

Melanie had a crush on Michael ever since middle school. Now that they were in high school she really wanted to be his girlfriend. When Michael started hanging out and smoking with friends she joined him and did not question him. Being with him was so important that she skipped some classes after lunch period to ride in his car with his new friends. When she was called into the school office by the principal and questioned she was nervous about being suspended. Her parents would be so disappointed in her.

This is an exaggerated example, but it could happen. **Maturity Test 2 is about building and maintaining healthy relationships.** In this example, the key item to focus on is that the D2W character Melanie did not look out for her own life. She was so focused on making Michael like her that she made irresponsible decisions that negatively affected her. Do you do that? **Are there some relationships in your life that are costing you? Are you mature in how you pick your friends and relationships?**

Later, you will be introduced to Goal 3 - Healthy Relationships in the D2W Steering Wheel. Think about it. Don't your parents ask you about your friends all the time? Don't they care about who you hang out with? Why do you think they care about whom you choose as friends? They understand that who you hang around will influence you either positively or negatively. You probably do not appreciate their concern always, but that means they care about you and where your life will end up. They care about your future. **Do not be naïve. Who you hang around will affect your life in some way.** We all affect each other. Maybe it is simply influencing your best friend to try out for the basketball team. Maybe your friends may try to get you to shoplift. Maybe your best friend is trying to get you to consider a spring vacation trip overseas with her family. Your values, choices, and even your beliefs are sometimes swayed and affected by the people around you. This is not only limited to only your friends, but can be your parents, siblings, or even neighbors. Healthy relationships extend to anyone you spend time with or listen to. This includes the organizations you are involved with.

What school clubs, churches, or organizations do you belong to? Whoever you spend time with will impact you in some way. **You are mature and responsible when you are aware of who is in your life and surround yourself with people and organizations that help not hurt your life.** Of course, that means you have to be a good friend yourself and demonstrate that you are someone who helps others to pursue their goals in life instead of hindering them. You are a real friend when you can be trusted to encourage others to make good choices for their life instead of influencing them to make wrong decisions that harm their life.

D2W Assignment: It's Your Turn

List five important people who support and believe in you. Identify their role in your life. Describe how they demonstrate their support, and you show your appreciation.

Person/Role in Your	How do they show	How do you show appreciation?
1. _____	_____	_____
2. _____	_____	_____
3. _____	_____	_____
4. _____	_____	_____
5. _____	_____	_____

Maturity Test 3: *Identifying and using resources*

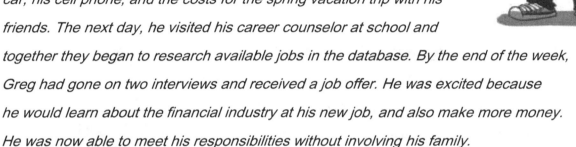

Greg had saved up more than $3,000 for his used car. He was excited.

He set a goal that he would have a car by his senior year.

He asked his dad to contribute the last $500 and he would pay him back

from his part-time job. Two weeks after he got his car, his supervisor

shared they were cutting back, and he would be let go. Greg had a lot of

responsibilities. He owed his dad, and he also was responsible for paying

$100 for car insurance, not to mention the gas and the oil changes for the

car, his cell phone, and the costs for the spring vacation trip with his

friends. The next day, he visited his career counselor at school and

together they began to research available jobs in the database. By the end of the week,

Greg had gone on two interviews and received a job offer. He was excited because

he would learn about the financial industry at his new job, and also make more money.

He was now able to meet his responsibilities without involving his family.

Test 3 involves identifying and using resources in a timely manner. This is a true test of maturity. In this scenario, Greg was not only aware of his responsibilities, but he figured out where to get the necessary information and resources to solve his dilemma. Greg did not procrastinate, but he sought out his career counselor as a resource to help him find a new job. Because of his mature attitude and diligent efforts, he was able to meet his  financial obligations without involving others. A major sign of maturity is handling money matters responsibly without delay. This test is not always related to money, but anything you need for your journey. When you have a goal or even a problem, you may need resources from other sources to help you. This could be scholarship information, job listings, community clubs, counselors, etc. Whatever you need, make a list of the resources and then be responsible for finding out how to get them.

Identify three resources either from your school, your neighborhood library, your church, and/or available community to help you accomplish your dreams or responsibilities.

Fill in your answers below.

	Resources	Why do you need them?	What actions do you need to take?
1.			
2.			
3.			

Maturity Test 4: *Making and standing by your decisions*

Antonio was so proud of himself. He had kept working out with his new fitness trainer for six weeks. He was following all the instructions from his nutritionist also. He had lost 20 lbs. in three weeks. He was focused and motivated to lose the next 60 lbs. While on spring vacation with his friends in Europe, everyone was telling him to relax and eat whatever he wanted. He thought that might be okay for a few days, but that meant days of eating pizza, nachos, and any junk food all day and night with everyone else. He did not want to even start. Everyone kept offering him junk food, but he kept on saying 'no' to foods he knew were no good for him. Surprisingly, Eliza noticed his resilience and made a big deal to support Antonio's decision and decided not to bring any unhealthy foods in the vacation house. For the rest of the vacation, everyone was eating healthy and even taking the time to get out and exercise. Antonio was grateful for Eliza's friendship and supporting his decision.

Test 4 is about making and standing by your decisions. It is not the easiest test to pass. Most people can make a decision, but can they stay true to their decision when it gets difficult? Life will check you out and see if you are serious about standing by your commitments and doing what is right for your life. Even when family members or friends challenge your resolve to stay steadfast, you need to do this for yourself. Your decisions should align with your dreams and goals and be supported by your character or behavior. You will make dozens of decisions in your lifetime and for various reasons. Some decisions are easy, and some are difficult. You will make decisions on what extracurricular activities to be involved in. You will make decisions on who to be close to and who your friends are. You will eventually make decisions on educational pursuits, career choices, and business opportunities.

One thing to look out for is when other people try to change your mind and manipulate you. **Sometimes we make decisions because our friends want us to. We do for others what we will not do for ourselves, which is protecting our interests and standing up for what we want and believe.** We need to be our own best friends. It takes a mature person to say "No" to peer pressure and stick by their decisions. Our decisions are just as important as anyone else's, and people who care about you will not consciously destroy your resolve. Stand your ground. They will respect you. You ultimately are responsible for the decisions you make. Life rewards decision-makers.

D2W Assignment: It's Your Turn

Write down what you have decided in the last weeks or months? Are you on track with your decisions? How can these decisions benefit your life? Answer the questions below.

What have you decided?	Are you on track?	How can it benefit you?
1. _____	_____	_____
2. _____	_____	_____
3. _____	_____	_____

These four maturity areas will continually be revisited throughout your life. Life will present different scenarios to you. If you study closely, you will find these tests will be repeated, but in more grown-up experiences. For example, Maturity Test 1 deals with handling responsibilities. This is a constant. You will always be challenged with managing your responsibilities for the rest of your life. As you mature, your responsibilities will become more complex. Today your responsibilities might be taking out the trash, but tomorrow as an adult it might be going to work and taking care of your family. Maturity Test 2 deals with relationships. You probably can recognize who your real friends are. As an adult, you will have to do the same thing, but hopefully, you will not be stressing over cheerleaders stealing your boyfriend like D2W Character Melanie. Maturity Test 3 deals with resources. You might be focused on trying to save money and buy a dress to the prom, but later, as an adult, you will need to find a home near your job. Lastly, Maturity Test 4 deals with making and standing by your decisions. As a young adult, you might be deciding which college major to choose or deciding whether to join the baseball or basketball team. Life demands that you make decisions and not keep changing your mind all the time. All these maturity tests qualify you for personal advancement to the next maturity level. You must understand their importance and demonstrate you are mature, committed to personal growth, and ready to master every experience you encounter.

D2W Stop Sign Alert

Try to recognize when you are facing Life's tests and do your best to qualify for your next opportunities. Understand how your behavior will impact the situation. If you want to be treated as a mature young adult and have more opportunities, you have to show you are ready. Hold yourself accountable. Realize your integrity is on the line. Make it your mission to be diligent to be prepared.

Chapter 4: Being Lost in the Fog

You are probably in the 'fog' about this title. When I refer to being 'lost in the fog,' I mean being confused about what you might want to do with your life; not knowing how to go about getting what you want; experiencing a lack of desire and motivation; or maybe even being discouraged about life. It happens to everyone at some point in their lives. Whatever the reason, when you are 'lost in the fog,' your vision is unclear, you cannot see clearly where you are in life, where you are going, or what you need to do next. You cannot see out of the windshield. If you have ever driven in the fog, it can be really scary. You cannot see the cars in front of you or on the side. Everyone is moving slowly, hopefully. If you do not pull to the side, you have to strain to see the car lights in front of you. You have to keep moving straight and be careful not to get out of your lane and crash into the other cars.

Does everyone experience these anxious feelings about their life? Just know this, everyone experiences these kinds of feelings at some point, but not to the same degrees. In fact, it usually doesn't happen just once, but you can find yourself experiencing the 'lost in the fog' feelings throughout your life at different times and for different reasons. **It will not last forever.** Many young people find themselves very lost and confused after high school and in college. Those who stay unfocused may find themselves like this for years after high school without a definite goal or purpose. Instead of this being an exciting time, some get overwhelmed with the anxiety and spiral into fear and depression. Sure, everyone knows it is expected to either go to college or find a job, but when you have no defined interest or passion, nothing makes sense to you. When you do not know your next move or you are between opportunities, life can be scary. You have that 'lost in the fog' feeling.

Why does the 'lost in the fog' experience happen? Being 'lost in the fog' is nobody's fault; it just happens and usually unexpectedly. One moment you feel great, and you pretty much have a handle on life and then that 'lost in the fog' experience comes over you. It is uncomfortable and scary because you are full of uncertainty. You do not have to do anything to experience this in your life. A lot of times it simply comes over you when you are growing and coming into a new place. Everyone is prone to experience these feelings when they need more clarity and direction, especially when evaluating new opportunities and making new decisions about their life.

What should you do when you are 'lost in the fog' and want to move ahead? You must **commit to building your vision to see clearly.** When you find yourself in this place, and I have several times before, the important thing you can do is get more perspective so you can see clearly. When you cannot see clearly where your life is headed, it is not the time to make new or big decisions that have the potential to change your life drastically. You have no perspective. You need more information. This is when you need to take it slowly.

You cannot allow yourself or others to force you into making hasty decisions. When you are 'driving in the fog,' you may not be able to pull over. ***What does that mean?* You have to stay with the decisions that are in place right now until the fog clears so you can carefully proceed.** Continue to get more information until you are in a 'clearer' place to make moves and decisions that work for your life.

If you have been involved in dance for years and now you are growing tired of it, do you continue or do you try out for something new? Do you go out for cheerleading, drama, or sports? What if you are ready to move on and break up with your boyfriend, but feel anxious about hurting him and not being in a relationship? What if all your friends have figured out what colleges they want to attend and you have no clue? It is time for self-reflection. Your understanding of who you are and what you want in life helps you get through those 'lost in the fog' moments. Realize when you are experiencing the 'lost in fog' moment and do not panic or retreat into depression. Research and seek the information on unfamiliar areas and, once you are confident and have enough information, make wise decisions. New areas and situations will challenge you and sometimes make you feel intimidated and unsure, but that is when you have the potential to grow as a person. You tap into personal strength by not being afraid of the unknown. **For every challenge, you need to be the challenger.** Stay connected to good friends and resources. Talk to someone you trust. Keep yourself active, stay open to exploring new interests, and give yourself time to reflect on your values. Build your perspective and vision by staying positive and open to new information. Be ready to proceed and maneuver ahead when you get the information that resonates with you.

D2W Character Scenario

It seemed like Antonio always knew he wanted to be a doctor. His sisters and brothers expected him to change his mind, but he never did. He focused on his academics, won scholarships, and got accepted to the best medical school in the country in his senior year. Tracy, his older sister, had already graduated from high school and was still struggling to make a decision for what she wanted to do with her life. She started community college, but dropped out the second year. She was envious of Antonio because he was so confident about his future and she was still unsure. When she read about Antonio's class assignment on 'What do you want to BE as an adult?' she thought she might ask Antonio what he learned. She was embarrassed to ask these life questions of her younger brother, but maybe it would help her make some decisions about her own life. Antonio was willing to share the information with Tracy. In fact, he introduced her to his mentor and Tracy was able to gain insight and perspective on some of her career interests and goals. This helped her alleviate a lot of self-doubt. She made a decision to go back to college and finish her education.

D2W Stop Sign Alert

It is important to stay encouraged and gain perspective as you move your life forward. When you are unclear and perplexed about where your life is headed, it is not the time to make hasty decisions. Be smart and do not lose patience. If you believe in yourself, keep exposing yourself to developmental opportunities and building your skills, you will gain focus on what you are most passionate about. Build your vision to see clearly toward your future.

What decisions are unclear right now? Are you perplexed about anything? Write down some things you need clarity on. Who could possibly give you information and guide you? What actions do you need to take and when will you start?

What do you need clarity on?	Who can support you?	What actions will you take and when?
1. _____	_____	_____
2. _____	_____	_____
3. _____	_____	_____

Chapter 5: Were You Raised with the 3C's: Caring, Competent, & Competitive?

When you leave your home to go off and start your adult life what is it that you need to leave home with? Some young people will be more prepared than others, but what are the essential character strengths and frame of mind that parents and guardians want to see built up in you? As adults, we want to see what I call the 3C's. We want to see young people who are **caring, competent, and competitive**. *Why are these qualities so important?* Without them, I believe young people will not advance well in our society as they would like and will not feel proud of themselves in the long run. These three standards are critical for you to be prepared to manage your life and confidently demonstrate your value in the community.

Why caring?

What happens when a young person is not a caring person? How does that affect them in the world? Also, how does that affect the people with whom they share their lives? Well, let's first look at what a caring person looks like. A caring young person listens to the needs of their parents, siblings, teachers, friends, neighbors, community, nation, and even world. They care about themselves and what is happening around them. They are connected.

If people cared more about each other how many of the world problems would be solved? There would be no loud noise disturbances where music is blasting at 2 am or 6 am in the morning. Senior citizens would not have to stand on a crowded bus in danger of falling if a caring young person was sitting nearby. As a society, we would not experience name-calling, bullying, or fighting on our school campuses. A neighbor in trouble could depend on their neighbor to phone the police, or a neighborhood creek would be cleaned up from concerned citizens.

I remember a true story about a young middle student that got in trouble at school. He had already been evaluated by school counselors as having "no empathy" for others in the classroom. He would continually disturb the other students by making a lot of noise, preventing them from doing their work. He would tease students incessantly. He had no respect for other people's property. He found himself in big trouble when he stole and defaced his teacher's baseball hat by writing on it with a black marker. He did not care how his behavior affected others. However, he felt personal pain when his dad made him pay the teacher $12.00 for the hat. I remember him saying, "But, Dad, that is my money. I saved it up to buy me something." He demonstrated selfish and uncaring behavior, but when it came to his personal needs, he expected others to be concerned. *Can you believe that?* He was completely disconnected with how his behavior affected others. How would it make you feel if someone did that to your property? There are plenty of people in the world that do not care for others and will harm you and feel no remorse. This example is an isolated event, but multiply this several times in our communities, and you find yourself in a world full of people that will take advantage of you, destroy your property, and not look back until it happens to them.

How can being a caring person help you advance in the world? A caring person has a huge advantage over an uncaring person. If you are a caring person, this character strength will work for you when you have a job. People like caring people, including your future supervisors. If you have ever worked at a job and asked someone to cover your shift, then you should understand how helpful it is for others to be caring and supportive. Others help you when they know you care. When you are a caring person and can think of others instead of just yourself, you feel better inside. You can feel the pain of a fellow student who lost their parent. You can feel the pain of a neighbor who is suffering physically. You can feel the pain of a friend who did not get the scholarship they needed. Being a caring person means you are emotionally connect to others and choose to understand and show compassion, and even sometimes help if you can. You will find this makes you feel good about yourself and also helps you believe there are people who will care and show you support when you need it. You get what you give. Be the kind of person who others can talk to and share their pain. Be a support to family and friends. You do not know when you will need the same kind of care.

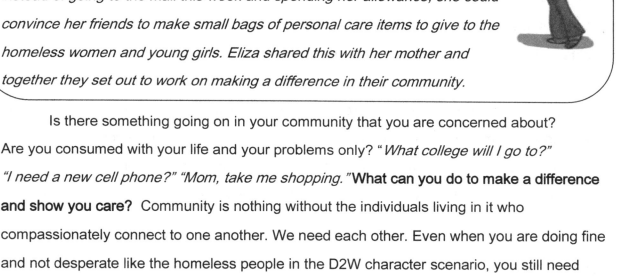

D2W Character Scenario

Eliza watched intently as the morning news show revealed the homeless situation in her community. Her family struggled with finances, but never like that. It almost brought her to tears when she saw a whole family with little kids sleeping on the streets. She pondered what she could do. Maybe instead of going to the mall this week and spending her allowance, she could convince her friends to make small bags of personal care items to give to the homeless women and young girls. Eliza shared this with her mother and together they set out to work on making a difference in their community.

Is there something going on in your community that you are concerned about? Are you consumed with your life and your problems only? *"What college will I go to?"* *"I need a new cell phone?" "Mom, take me shopping."* **What can you do to make a difference and show you care?** Community is nothing without the individuals living in it who compassionately connect to one another. We need each other. Even when you are doing fine and not desperate like the homeless people in the D2W character scenario, you still need other people to care about your life, right? Well, it starts with you. **Make sure you are a caring person, and you demonstrate that concern beyond your own personal needs.** That is a winner. That's being D2W.

Why competent?

Remember when you were playing softball or some other sport and the leaders were selecting who they wanted to be on their teams? As the best kids one-by-one were being selected you just stood there hoping to be called. *Mike. I got Larry. Billy. Michelle. I pick Lisa. When would your name be called? You prayed nervously not to be the last kid called. Your name was called finally.* **What was happening in this example?** You were being sized up for your skills. *Could you catch the ball? Were you one of the strongest hitters? Could you run and get on the base? Would you help your team win?* Competence is about your skills.

Competence is a word you normally see on a report card indicating the skill level of a student. When we ask if someone is competent, we are asking if they know, understand, and can perform in a certain area. *Are you competent at Geometry? Do you know what a trapezoid is? Can you manipulate and understand theorems? Are you a strong chess player? Are you an excellent writer? Are you a skilled musician?* Basically, are you knowledgeable and skilled? Whether your competence is attained from traditional schooling, reading books, participating in programs, it is something you do well and where you have some level of mastery.

It is essential for you to graduate high school mastering the basic academic competencies. Writing. Reading. Arithmetic. *What is the value of your education if you do not learn how to do these basic things?* I come from a family where your communication was constantly corrected if you slipped and butchered the English language. That is what I get for having a mother who majored in English in college. One day I was reading a letter from a person in a supervisory position leading other employees. The email was filled with grammatical errors that anyone who passed 8th grade English would immediately take out their red pen. As I read his email, I was embarrassed and saddened that there are many people without adequate writing skills. Writing is just one area of performance. There are hundreds of areas that demand that you become competent if you want to be taken seriously in your career, business, and life in general.

What if you could not write your name? How limiting would that be? Okay, I know you can write your name. *Can you speak clearly and make a presentation without saying 'umm' or 'you know' every sentence? Can you write an essay and communicate your ideas without a whole lot of grammatical errors and confusing sentence structures? Can you lead a team on a project and make sure you meet the deadlines? What am I saying? Do you have skills? Are you competent? What can you do and are you any good at it?* These are a lot of questions, but answer them for yourself. I am a big believer in a person knowing what they are skilled at and being confident enough to let others know. I did not describe a conceded person. Big difference. You will need to speak about your skills at job interviews. This itself is a skill. Let's look at D2W Character Antonio and discover the things he is good at.

D2W Character Scenario

Antonio was always labeled the smart kid. He sure was not the athlete. At 30 pounds overweight, he was bullied and teased all throughout middle school. He knew it was something he needed to work on, but right now he was focusing on his recent big win at the national junior chess competition. He won first place and a $500 scholarship. He was excited. His Trigonometry teacher said his superior math skills were the secret for his success in chess. For Antonio, math came easy. He was smart and competent, and doing well in school and winning national trophies in chess was important to him.

At this moment in your life, you may not fully understand or appreciate how all the school subjects you have been exposed to will assist you in life. You might be saying to yourself that school is a waste of time. Not everyone has a love affair with school. That's just honest. However, you need to realize that you are not wasting your time in school because it is the foundation of your knowledge and you can use it to springboard into greater learning opportunities. There is a lot to be said when a young person has it together and is intelligent. *Why?* They can think and reason. They can compare and contrast data and form opinions. You might not be the smartest or even the most successful, but when you are competent, it shows. When you are ignorant and lack skills, it also shows. Other people will acknowledge your capabilities and hard work, and more opportunities will come your way.

You need to be competent in other things besides academics though. You need to be competent in social things also like "handling your business." *What do I mean by that?* I mean having the ability to arrange your class schedule, pay your bills, sign up for the DMV test, and send in your grades and academic portfolio to the colleges you are interested in. Some young people struggle with their ability to organize themselves or become frustrated and baffled with these other life responsibilities. You have heard people say, "She's smart, but she has no common sense." They are saying there are some life skills that are missing. Just make sure you have it going on intellectually and also on the social side.

Why competitive?

Some young people are born competitors. They compete for being the best Frisbee thrower, the best baseball hitter, or even the best Nintendo gamer. They even compete for their parents' attention. That's a larger issue. However, some young people are not great competitors. Whatever the case, you cannot survive in this world without learning to be competitive. Everywhere you look there is a competition. When it comes to scholarships for college, applying for a summer job, or finding the love of your life, you have to be ready and prepared to compete. Do not be naïve.

Competition has a lot to do with your preparation and skill level, but it also has a lot to do with your mental attitude. You have heard the saying, "If you think like a winner, you will be one." Most people win in life because they desire it more than others. They may not be the strongest or brightest, but because they had a competitive mindset, focused their efforts, and wanted it more than the next person, they won. All sports players know that playing the game just to play is not the goal. You want to win. **Being competitive and having a mindset to be the best at what you do is the starting blocks to personal power. Own your gifts and talents. Be brilliant and do not be afraid to show it.**

Greg was the shortest kid on his block. He was always the last one to be picked when the neighborhood kids played basketball. It was not that he was not a decent player. He hustled better that all of them, but just because of his size his friends thought he was no good. He experienced this all through elementary school, but when he went to middle school, things changed. He joined his school's basketball team. His dad paid for him to attend basketball clinics.

He noticed that his coach was shorter than the other male teachers and he wondered how he won so many championships in his college basketball days. One day he mustered up the courage to ask his coach about his experiences being shorter than most basketball players. His coach looked at him and put his hand on his shoulder and said, "It is true that a basketball player is always judged on his height. If you are not very tall, you will have to show more tenacity and determination than everyone else. That was all the encouragement Greg needed. From that day forward, he knew he could make a difference if he was competitive. He was never the last one picked again.

How do the 3Cs work together? There is no way you will be competitive at anything if you do not act like a winner or champion and also think like one. If you have no confidence in your skills, you will cower when it is time to compete. People who go after opportunities are confident about what they can do. This is attractive, and people see it on you. People like to help and make friends with caring people. When you are caring, competent, and competitive, you have the right combination to be successful. When opportunities like a theater play lead, cheerleader captain position, or career opportunity presents itself, the 3Cs will work to your advantage. Not everyone was raised with the 3Cs. Not everyone cares about you or your feelings. Not everyone challenges their mediocrity and build skills. Others are afraid of competition. **Remember, success is your ability to harness your genius and brilliance to serve other valuable people and to create something greater than yourself.**

D2W Stop Sign Alert

You should always be growing as a person. Understand how your gifts and talents can help you have a successful life and also connect to others in your community. Your life is not just meant for yourself. Increase your knowledge and abilities and become irreplaceable and not obsolete. Others will seek you out when you become an invaluable asset.

D2W Assignment: It's Your Turn

Write down what you care about and how you demonstrate it. Write down areas you are skilled in and how you can improve. Write down the areas that you are competitive in and how your achievements have built your confidence.

I care about these things.　　　　　　How do you demonstrate that you are caring?

1. ————————————————　　————————————————

I am skilled and capable in these areas.　　How can you improve your skills?

2. ————————————————　　————————————————

I am competitive in these areas.　　How has your confidence improved?

3. ————————————————　　————————————————

Chapter 6: The 3C's to Personal Disaster: Crashes, Collisions, and Catastrophes

In life, we can find ourselves in places of serious personal challenge. **I call these experiences crashes, collisions, and catastrophes.** Now, there is a chapter later in the book called the 4Ds on a destructive road. This lesson deals with your individual actions that create negative experiences. It does not involve others. **Crashes, collisions, and catastrophes are different.** The 3C experiences do not mean you necessarily did anything wrong. Sometimes it might be your fault, somebody else's, or just something that happened that could not be avoided. Just think about it. A car crash can come at the most inconvenient time.

How many of you have been in a fender bender, a minor car crash, or even a life and death car accident? It could be out of your control and have nothing to do with the consequences of your decisions. In fact, you might be doing everything right.

Crash experiences are when you hit something. Now, crashes involve only you; others are not affected. *You hit a wall. You scrape the bumper.* This is a minor experience, not a tragic one. You are still alive, but maybe a little shaken up with some personal damage. It is more than a problem, but it should not devastate your life. An example might be breaking your arm and missing your football championship game. It affects only you. It could devastate you if your life is about football like our D2W character Michael. It is more than a problem, but it is an example of a "crash" when your life is damaged by the experience. If you remember the D2W character Janice who desires to be a professional ballet dancer, her life would be crushed if she did not get picked for the ballet recital. Another crash example would be if you were dropped from the basketball team because you did not keep your grades up. These are not near-death experiences. They are hurtful experiences, not the best of circumstances, but they don't have to ruin your life. You can pick yourself up, fix some things, and keep motivated toward your goals. These are 'crashes' where your life hits the wall not involving anyone else. It is a negative experience, but life continues.

Collisions are negative experiences that involve others. These experiences involve other people and how you interact with them. It may be your fault or maybe someone else's. For our purposes, we are defining the word 'collision' as an accident usually more detrimental than a crash. Collisions are described as a major accident involving others. Cars hit each other in the intersection. Your brakes go out. You slam into the car in front of you. Those are collisions. If you experience a collision you "collide" or slam up against somebody else and have problems with them. Here are some examples. You get into a nasty argument with your best friend and break up because she believes you were flirting with her boyfriend. You get distracted on the bus after the football game, and your cell phone is missing. You accuse the person sitting behind you and get into a fight. You are short $120 for your senior pictures, so you decide to take $120 from the register at your job and replace it when you get paid, but your supervisor finds out and fires you. You listen to your boyfriend and stay after your curfew and your car gets pulled over by the police and you are jailed for drunk driving. These are all examples of collision experiences. They are pretty serious for a young person. Sometimes your lack of judgment, selfishness, or inappropriate behavior creates negative experiences for yourself and others. *What can you learn from these experiences?* **Be careful how you interact with other people.** You could be the catalyst or reason someone fails or succeeds. *Is your presence helping or hurting their chances to realize their dreams? Are the people in your life better because they know you?* **Make it your goal and commitment to strengthening people in your life, not weakening them.**

Catastrophes, just as the word suggests, are those near-death situations you never want to experience. They could end your life or seriously alter it. This could be a head-on accident. If you live through the experience and recover, you are fortunate. In life, some people go through tragedy and get stuck and never recover, meaning they are never the same. Their zest for life is gone, dreams and goals are ripped right out of their heart, and their confidence is so shaken they cannot find their way. I hope you never experience this level of devastation, but it does happen. Some people do not make it alive or walk away from these catastrophe experiences unharmed. This sounds pretty heavy for a book about young people living successful lives. Even, some young people endure challenging situations at their young age.

If one of your parents became ill unexpectedly, it could absolutely change the direction of your life. Being confined to a wheelchair after a major accident could block you emotionally for years, challenging you to figure out how to live the rest of your life. If this happened to you and you were a serious young athlete wanting to make it professionally, it could destroy you. A serious health problem could shake your world and make you question your future. These types of catastrophes require the strongest character to keep believing for better days. *Would you be strong enough to endure these extreme hardships? Would your life be devastated? How would you survive and keep your hope to live?* Seriously, stop a moment and ask yourself how you would recover from these experiences. *It's hard, isn't it?* Nobody wants to face these extreme tough times.

When you experience catastrophes, Life is speaking to you. Life is staring you in the face to see what you are made of. *Will he crumble? Is he tough enough for this?* Anyone who has been challenged by these types of devastating experiences knows exactly what I am talking about. I do not know what you have gone through in your young life. I know you have had some unpleasant experiences. Everyone has some level of these experiences. You might have escaped these really big ones at this point, and hopefully, you can live the rest of your life without experiencing severe catastrophes.

Whatever the case, this chapter is dedicated to giving you hope beyond all the negative 3C experiences. **You must understand that what is inside of you must be stronger than anything you face on the outside.** That is not just some motivational talk. The fact that you lived through the negative circumstances means there is an opportunity for restoration. I believe the 3C experiences, whether crashes, collisions, and catastrophes, may devastate us, but if we seek and keep reaching up, we will find strength to recover. I believe a person who wants to live again will find what they need to be revived. Even when you go through the toughest times, and you feel like your life is over, it is not. As long as you have breath in you, there is a chance to be strengthened again.

When we are going through these 3C experiences, we do not appreciate them. We are not thinking, *"This is going to make me a stronger person and help me to stand up for what I believe."* We feel the pain of the experiences. We are living it. The failure, the humiliation, the loss – all those things are real. *So, what can you do with this information?* Life is not for wimps. It demands that you be courageous. It is for those braving the storms of Life refusing to let go of their dreams regardless of what stands in their way. Period. You will be challenged. You will be tested. **Remember that if you keep building your character, you will be strong enough to endure and recover from any experience. Great people survive all kinds of losses, and they keep standing and pushing forward even with tears in their eyes.**

D2W Character Scenario

Eliza was waiting in the doctor's office by herself when her mother and doctor entered the room. They both looked sad and strange. Eliza could not wait any longer and inquired how bad it was. Her energy had been low for the last month, and she was experiencing some new pains, but she just thought it was the long hours of studying and being exhausted from working on the weekend at her intern position for the Mayor's office. She couldn't believe the doctor said the word 'cancer.' She had to start chemotherapy treatment quickly. It was devastating. Her life was about to change. She just had received the good news about her internship. Now what? She did not know anybody personally who ever went through what she was about to go through, especially anybody her age.

D2W Assignment: It's Your Turn

Write down any personal disasters you have experienced in your life. Identify which 3C personal disaster it was (crash, collision, or catastrophe). Identify how you recovered?

My personal disaster was…	3C Experience?	How did you recover?
1. _____	_____	_____
2. _____	_____	_____
3. _____	_____	_____

D2W Stop Sign Alert

It is not fun experiencing setbacks, personal failure, or tragedy. Think back on the last experience that you thought you would never recover from. It is now a part of your past experiences. Realize that the 3C experiences are to be faced, but they will not last forever. Commit to being stronger and wiser from every experience. See yourself strong and build your mental stamina for any challenge.

Chapter 7: Buckle Up: It's Time to Drive

Are you ready to buckle up and drive? No doubt you are ready to leave the passenger seat and hop into the driver's seat. It should be an exciting time in your life. You are getting closer to crossing over to being the adult you have dreamed about. All your learning and preparation has been for the next years of your life. I want to encourage you to be excited about your life. There are so many things to learn and experience. Do not let anxiety and fear rob you of this important time. Take every day to appreciate your life. When you think of your life, I want you to dream and visualize what great things are coming your way. No limits. No ceilings. *Are you excited about the possibilities?* The script for your life has not been written. Whatever you have experienced in school so far, whatever personal relationships and experiences you have had up to this point, use it for what it is worth. **Nothing defines you except your own mind.** You are creating your vision every day. Your life is about to take shape. *What do you see for your life?* It's all about looking out of that windshield and seeing and believing your life is headed toward great paths. **Buckle Up.** You are about to go on a ride. I have said enough. Oh, that's right. Before you take the wheel, there are a few more things to share with you. Keep reading.

D2W Character Scenario

School break was almost here. It couldn't come fast enough. Everyone was excited about the spring break trip to Europe. This was going to be a trip of a lifetime. You could not have put together a more diverse group. Janice, Melanie, and Eliza had different personalities, dreams, and ambitions, but they really cared for each other. Michael, Greg, and Antonio were opposites also, but this year they got much closer as everyone shared about their dreams and goals. This school year was definitely a time to find out what the next years would be like. Everyone was a little anxious, but they were more excited about the next chapters in their life after high school.

D2W Stop Sign Alert

Do not take this time for granted. There is so much possibility. Your future is yet to be determined. This is a crucial time for you to understand how precious life is. Be aware of how life gets formed. Each day matters. Each decision is important. There are plenty of people wishing they could go back and redo some things in their lives. Make a beautiful life for yourself. It's up to you. It's your time!!!

D2W Assignment: It's Your Turn

What are you most excited about the years ahead? List three things.

<u>I am excited about these things.</u>

1. _____

2. _____

3. _____

It's time to get on the road.

Are YOU Ready?

The Road Starts Now.

Now it's time to introduce the D2W Life Management System. In this part of the book, we now transition to the 20 powerful life lessons. There are three sections. Section One is called 'Life Is a Journey, Not a Trip.' It has five chapters. Section Two is called 'The Driver's Handbook.' It has four chapters. Section Three is called 'Tools for Life.' It has 11 chapters.

When you read these chapters, visualize your mentor speaking wise words to you so you will be prepared for your journey. Your mentor believes in you and is excited about your future success. This is your opportunity to listen and learn because life comes really fast when you are in the "driver's seat." The more prepared you are, the better your journey will be. Use this information as your roadmap to guide you forward. That is exactly what it is. It is your D2W roadmap to success in life. **Are YOU Driven 2 Win? Are YOU D2W?**

Section One:

LIFE IS A JOURNEY, NOT A TRIP

Understanding that life is a journey and not a single trip is vital to living successfully. A journey requires more planning, more time, more resources, and a long-range view. Anyone can take a trip, but a journey toward your future endeavors will challenge you for the rest of your life. Life is a series of experiences or paths, roads, and highways. Life has a multitude of experiences to offer. Our lives are not formed by just one road or experience, but all of our travels are merged into a single life. All these paths create what is called your personal journey. The success of your personal journey is not merely measured by the destination, but the value of the experiences. What we eventually create is a lifetime of experiences, not simply the destination. The destination is 10% of living; the journey is the other 90%.

This insight empowers us to take charge and map out the direction of our lives. It also encourages us to prevent individual experiences from dominating the entirety of our lives, whether positive or negative. We have the power to visualize and shape our own life. As you drive your life forward believing the "sky is the limit," make sure you are enjoying the journey.

Lesson 1: Your DREAM is Your Journey

We all have dreams. We all want to accomplish great things and live to say, *"I did this or that."* *Who doesn't want to succeed in life and feel proud of themselves?* **Everyone has a dream and a purpose. Everyone desires to unlock the dream (for their lives) and experience personal satisfaction.** It is not enough to look at everyone else succeeding in life, getting into the best colleges, getting the scholarships, securing the internships, being fit, strong, and healthy, or traveling with their families on awesome vacations. Everyone wants their dreams to come true and wants to be proud of their lives. Don't you want good things for yourself? What do you dream about? What do you want out of your life? What are you willing to work hard for and achieve? Have you ever sat down and made a list of the things and experiences you want for your life? If you have, that is great. Keep doing that. If not, here is your chance.

Do this now. Take out a piece of paper. List 5 to 10 things you want for yourself. You should be able to do this in less than three minutes. There are three questions to ask yourself to start **"unlocking your dreams"** and **"igniting the passion"** for your life.

Question 1: What do you want to BE? Doesn't everyone ask you this question? I have two daughters. My youngest daughter was so tired of me asking her this question. You should have seen her face. *"Mom, you always ask me this. Could you please STOP?"* She went from considering a career as a business marketing professional to a nutritionist in the span of about one year. You have to keep asking the question until something sticks. Answer the question for yourself. **What do you want to BE?** Some young people believe they know what career and/or business they want to pursue. Some do not. They are still investigating life. That is good. Keep seeking and finding what fits. Most people in high school are not exactly sure what they want to be. Even years later, they may still be searching for what feels right. If you don't know what you want to be, you probably know what you DO NOT want to be. *"I do not want to be a forest ranger." "I do not want to be an accountant." "I do not want to be a horse trader."* Now, if you want to pursue these careers, go for it. It just shows you that narrowing your choices by understanding what careers or businesses you do not want to pursue is a valid way to discover your dreams.

I remember that after my first accounting class in community college, I knew for certain I did not want to be an accountant. I did not want to count numbers and check boxes for the rest of my life. The discipline, the forms, the rigid structure was more than I could stand. I could get a good grade, but it was not something I liked doing and would not be a career choice. I was not interested at all. I had a friend from high school who went to the same community college with me, and she loved accounting. She was excited to take all the accounting classes she could. I didn't. She obviously had the constitution or personality to do this kind of work all day. My emphatic 'NO' took one more decision off the map for me. You can use the same process of elimination. Years later, I "fell" into working in the accounting department after I finally finished my Bachelor's degree and my supervisor took me to his side after about four years being there and said, *"Your gifting is not here. You are called somewhere else."* That was brutally honest. It was a job. I learned a lot, I did the work, but my passion and zest for life kept trying to get out and live. Basically, he was confirming what I already knew when I was in my early 20's. **So again, what do you want to BE?** If you do not know how to sincerely answer this question right now, keep experiencing life and expanding your options and one day you will be able to come close to what feels right.

What do you want to HAVE? The lifestyle you grew up with leaves an impression on what you want and what you do not want. You might be saying, *"I want a successful career and not just a low-paying job." "I want to travel around the world."* The lifestyle you saw your parents create might have a major influence on you. If they finished their college degrees and attained successful careers, then you might hold yourself to this same standard. You might be saying *"I want to have nice things like cars, homes, great clothes, go on fabulous vacations, and afford the things I want."* You might want to be married and have a large family or not. Whatever you see at your age can influence what you want to have as an adult. Even if you were challenged financially and your family struggled, these experiences could motivate you to work diligently to create better circumstances in your life. Regardless of positive or negative experiences, you are making observations and decisions on what you want to create for your life. Your task is to start visualizing and thinking about your values and priorities. Even at your age, where you are right now, begin making a list of what you want to have and figure out if they are important enough to really put effort toward acquiring them. Do not make the mistake of being impatient. We are talking about your whole life. You cannot have everything now, but as you "pace yourself" and show maturity, you will be rewarded for your efforts. Remember it took your parents or other adults a lifetime of hard work to acquire the things you admire. Do not think that you can get them automatically without effort. Prioritize. Pace yourself.

There is one more question. **What do you want to EXPERIENCE?** The answer to this question might be related to the same areas as the other two questions. For example, if you decided you want to have an exciting career, you might want to experience traveling for your career. If you answered that you want to have a healthy body, then you might want to experience hiking in beautiful countries. Do you get the point? These three questions work together and help you start dreaming and exploring the opportunities available to you. These questions force you to think bigger, become clear on what you want for yourself, and shape the life you want to live.

D2W Character Scenario

Michael wanted to be a professional football star. Janice wanted to be a professional ballet dancer. Antonio always knew that he wanted to be a pediatrician because he loved being a big brother and working with little kids. Melanie had no idea what she wanted to be. Everyone joked that she would inherit the family business, but that wasn't her dream. Greg bragged about his dream every chance he could get. He was the next billionaire. He was always pitching some new business to make money, but being patient and diligent was something he had to learn. Eliza was confident that she would be successful, but it was a toss-up between being a news reporter or a politician since she was so passionate about her community. The D2W crew was young, but they had plenty of time to figure it all out...or did they?

It is okay if you have not figured out all the answers to the questions. The important thing is to start thinking about it now, not later. Start understanding what you are good at and how you like to spend your time. *What could you see yourself doing as an adult that would be cool and you could be proud of?* Your dreams not only involve your career or business pursuits, but also what kind of life you want to create for yourself. You are in the driver's seat. Make the most of this time when you are young. Do not limit yourself. You have options and opportunities. **DREAM BIG. DARE TO DREAM DREAMS NOBODY HAS DARED BEFORE.** Do not sell yourself short. You need to read all those success stories about famous people. Business people. Actors. Sports giants. Presidents. Whatever profession, most people did not come from big money or affluence. They are regular people who persisted with their dreams to the point that now we recognize them for their brilliance, talent, creativity, and intelligence. That could be you. That could be me. We have what it takes to make our dreams a reality. At least we are on our way and moving into position, so we can live the dream. You only get one life. Make it a GREAT one. So, again, **what do you want to BE? What do you want to HAVE? What do you want to EXPERIENCE?**

D2W Stop Sign Alert

A journey is much longer than a trip. It consists of several trips. Find out what life has to offer. It is best to gain as much exposure as possible so you can be aware of all your options. Before you start your journey and make the mistake of setting your sights on a definite path, enjoy and experience life. Enjoy the journey!!!

<u>D2W Assignment: It's Your Turn</u>

Fill out a DREAM Cloud for each question?

What do I want to BE?	**What do I want to HAVE?**	**What do I want to EXPERIENCE?**

I want to be _____   My motive is _____

I want to have _____   My motive is _____

I want to experience _____   My motive is _____

Lesson 2: Three Questions for A Successful Journey

As you discover your dreams, there are three questions you have to ask yourself if you are going to make your dreams a reality. *Where am I NOW? Where am I GOING? What do I NEED to get there?* Without any dreams, these three questions are meaningless. That is why it is so important for you to protect your dreams and not limit your potential. <u>Your life begins to take shape once you believe your dreams are possible.</u> If you place a point on a piece of paper for Question 1 (**Where am I NOW?**) and then place another point for Question 2 (**Where am I GOING?**), you have a straight line. You have a road to lead you from where you are currently to where you are going. *Do you see the simplicity?* Now, the next question, Question 3 (**What do I NEED to get there?**) helps you create a list of items and resources you will need to accomplish what you desire. This list is called a needs assessment. When you ask yourself the three questions, you are referencing each DREAM Cloud you want for your life. The process is linking the questions in Lessons 1 and 2 together and start mapping out your personal journey. It is that simple. Answer the questions. It is important to write your answers on a paper and see your personal journey visually. You could do it in your mind somewhat, but when you put your dreams on paper, you are setting the course for your life right before your eyes.

Your dreams are not just going to fall into your lap or fall out of the sky. You have to go after your dreams with dedication and focus. **You have to define what you want in life and plan the path to go get it.** We do not always get everything we have planned, but at least having a plan helps us to be more successful and stay focused. This is how you plan your life. When you cannot answer the three questions, then you stay stuck and cannot move forward. You cannot focus. Your efforts are scattered instead of being organized. **Your dreams stay in the sky instead of being converted into manageable goals. Dreams are nothing more than clouds in the sky until you are ready to put in real effort, develop goals, and perform actions that translate into success.** The 'Three Questions on a Successful Journey' creates a road toward fulfilling your dreams.

Here is an example of how this works. Take DREAM Cloud Question 1. **What do you want to be?** *I want to be an engineer.* Lesson 2 Question. **Where am I NOW?** *I have researched the colleges and universities known for producing great engineers.* Next Question. **Where am I GOING?** *I am going to college for a Bachelor's degree in engineering. I will start a career at an engineering firm.* Question 3: **What do I NEED to get there?** *I need to take advanced mathematics courses. I need to find mentors in the engineering career industry. I need to attend summer STEM engineering camps and apply for scholarships.* This is how it works. This might not be your career choice, but whatever your dreams are you simply write out the answers the same way.

Your dreams might be related to your personal interests, academic and career pursuits, your friendships and relationships, and even your commitment to being healthy. The subject or area will change, but the questions remain the same. Question 1 **(Where am I Now?)** deals with your current knowledge and achievements. It is your starting place. It identifies where you are currently on the road. Question 2 **(Where am I going?)** deals with what you ultimately want to accomplish, but also includes the individual accomplishments along the way. It identifies where you want to go on the road. Question 3 **(What do you need to get there?)** deals with all the resources you need to be successful in pursuit of your dream.

Let's evaluate the dreams of D2W Character Janice. **What do you want to BE?** *I want to be a professional ballerina.* **Where are you NOW?** *I have trained for six years as a ballerina. I have been in eight ballet recitals. I have been the lead ballerina in two school productions.* **Question 2: Where am I GOING?** *I will continue lessons with my ballet instructor. I will audition for a scholarship to the top professional ballet school in New York after high school.* **Question 3: What do I need to get there?** *I need to hire a dedicated ballet teacher who will train me to get ready for my audition. I need to save up $1,500 to go to a prestigious ballet training camp this summer.* Now, these answers are only for one DREAM Cloud, which is related to Janice's passion for ballet. There are other DREAM Clouds to consider. Below is a DREAM Cloud chart with the questions from Lessons 1 and 2 to demonstrate how Janice would prepare her road.

		THREE QUESTIONS FOR A SUCCESSFUL JOURNEY		
DREAM Cloud Questions	*Answer*	Where am I NOW?	Where am I GOING?	What do I NEED to get there?
What do I want to Be?	*Professional ballet dancer* *JANICE*	I have trained for six years as a ballerina. I have been in eight ballet recitals and have had the lead part in two school productions.	I am going to the best professional ballet school in New York City after high school. This fall school year I am going to audition for a traveling ballet company and be home-schooled.	I need to hire a dedicated ballet teacher to train for the audition. I need to save up $1,500 dollars to go to the prestigious ballet summer camp.

What do I want to Have?	*Part-time job*	I have filled out five job applications.	I am going to work part-time after school and weekends to save money for ballet camp.	I need the following: resume, interviews, and business suit.
What do I want to Experience?	*Traveling around the world*	I have been to three countries (Australia, Canada, and Mexico).	I will visit Europe as a foreign exchange student.	I need the following: passport, money, and acceptance to traveling ballet company.

These essential questions are <u>only</u> necessary for people that want something greater in their life than what they currently have. *Is that you? What are your dreams and goals? Are you willing to go after them?* Ask yourself the three questions and write down your answers. *Do you want a successful career or business?* Ask the three questions.
Do you want to experience traveling to several countries? What do you need to get there? Make a list. *I need a passport. I need to save some money. I need to research countries to visit with friends.* This is how you win in life. You are not too young to start visualizing and considering what you want to create for your life. This is how you do it. Make your dreams come true. Be Driven 2 Win. Be D2W.

D2W Stop Sign Alert

Some of you are so excited to get on the road and start driving. Well, slow down because, before you get started, you need to plan your path. Do not go in circles or be sidetracked. There are many things to achieve and experience along the journey. Sometimes the next road to take is not clear, but if you have an idea of where you are going, the journey will be much more successful.

<u>D2W Assignment: It's Your Turn</u>

Rewrite your answers to the three DREAM Clouds. Write down the answers to

'The Three Questions for a Successful Journey' below to create your road.

What do I want to BE?
What do I want to HAVE?
What do I want to EXPERIENCE?

 DREAM CLOUD 1

 DREAM CLOUD 2

 DREAM CLOUD 3

		THREE QUESTIONS FOR A SUCCESSFUL JOURNEY		
DREAM Cloud Questions	*Answer*	Where am I NOW?	Where am I GOING?	What do I NEED to get there?
What do I want to Be?				
What do I want to Have?				
What do I want to Experience?				

Lesson 3: Three Highways of Learning

Do you believe learning is over when school is over? I hope not. It is just the beginning. Learning is more than English, Algebra, or Biology class. **Learning is about embracing the opportunity to expand yourself and being exposed to new possibilities.** What we learn becomes a part of who we are. <u>Learning is depicted as highways, not merely roads.</u> Highways are longer travel passages than roads because you can go faster and farther as you pursue your dreams. **Knowledge, skills, and experiences are highways that advance your life forward.** The 'Three Highways of Learning' is similar to a resume. It details all of the highways of learning you have traveled. A resume details your knowledge, skills, and experiences related to professional and volunteer involvements. Normally, we only are concerned about a resume when we want to get a job, but you must understand the value beyond that single purpose. What knowledge have you obtained? What skills have you learned and demonstrated? What valuable experiences have you lived that helps you to become a better informed and capable person? *If you are not willing to learn, no one can help you. If you are willing to learn, no one can stop you. (Kathy Jeffers) Never stop learning because Life never stops teaching. Being ignorant is not much of a shame, as being unwilling to learn. (Benjamin Franklin)* I love these quotations. They challenge your commitment to learning. Become the best person you can be by continually challenging yourself to be exposed to new learning opportunities. Be a life learner.

Knowledge

Knowledge is an essential highway to advance your life. **Knowledge is defined as the attainment of facts, truths, or principles from study or investigation.** What do you know? Do you sit with excitement in your History class? Can you recite the latest historical events as if they happened in your lifetime? It is so remarkable to see a young person that cannot remember anything shared in their History class, but can recite every fact about their favorite basketball or football players. They can mesmerize you with the latest current events for hours. Are you fascinated with Art and considering an Art degree in college? Do you know the latest hip-hop artists, their music, and the story of their lives? What is your mind filled with that you want more of? Knowledge comes in all kinds of forms, and it also comes from different places. We all want knowledge; however, our interests point us toward the knowledge we seek. You are acquiring knowledge when you pick up a newspaper and read about your community. You are acquiring knowledge when you visit a museum or listen with interest to a political debate. Do you have a fascination with fashion and always have your nose in a fashion magazine or looking at a television show on fashion? What are you curious about? What things would you like to learn more about?

I encourage you to be open to learning many new things and surround yourself with information about all kinds of areas to find what really interests you. Music, animals, cars, politics, dance or sports are only a few areas that you can accumulate knowledge in. It just might be the highway you need to travel on to reach your next destinations.

We make the mistake of limiting learning to only what happens in the classroom. It is so much more than that. **You devote your elementary, middle school, and high school years and possibly six or more years of college to your formal education.** *Do you realize your schooling is probably no more than 20 years, which represents only 25% of your life?* You will need to learn more than what formal schooling provides. Your formal education is the initial highway to advance your life forward, but there is more. People who finish professional degrees are usually more financially stable than others most of the time. This is one valid reason why following through with your education is so important.

Here's an assignment. Ask your parents about their 'Three Highways of Learning.' In fact, ask three other adults if any distractions got in the way of their continuing and finishing their formal education. Many start pursuing college degrees after high school, but it is easy to get distracted and drop out. Relationships, jobs, bills and other responsibilities are examples of things that can steal your attention away from finishing your formal education. Be diligent. Watch out for the pitfalls. Other priorities and commitments will try to get in the way of your learning. Do not let them. Keep on track. See the knowledge highway in front of you and keep driving until you get to where you want to go.

Remember that the ultimate goal is not to get good grades. Being engaged where you grow as a person should be the ultimate goal. *Don't let schooling interfere with your education. (Mark Twain)* Your education is more than just school. **Do not fall into the trap of measuring yourself and limiting your potential for the rest of your life based on how well you did in school.** Some students believe they are 'dumb' because they struggled or did not earn high grades in formal school. If you are not careful, you could let academic failures shape what you believe about yourself as a learner. Many people make their school life a defining point and cannot seem to move past it. Being voted as the 'Most Likely to Succeed' or the 'Best Dressed' in high school should not be your biggest accomplishment and will have no meaning or value once you walk across that high school graduation stage. Although your grade point average is important for creating academic opportunities in your life, it should not be the pinnacle of your life. There are bigger things to accomplish and learn.

For example, like the D2W Character Janice, you might have a keen interest in dance, and your dance teacher suggests you read an autobiography of a famous dancer. It is not a required class assignment, but you do it because your interest in dance is so big you want to learn as much as possible. You not only want to dance, but you are also interested in researching the lives of others who have done what you want to do. The learning we gain through studying, listening to class lectures, and reading books is foundational knowledge. It is a foundation; it is a starting place. Having knowledge in Algebra, English literature, and History sets the stage for more learning. You must go on and acquire additional knowledge that will add to your foundation. What if you are highly committed to basketball, and in your business class you have a research paper due on a famous business person? You might connect your interest in basketball and your knowledge of business and write an essay on Magic Johnson, his basketball career, and also how he became a well-established businessman transforming several communities. Find out what inspires you and learn as much as you can. You will be amazed how much you seek knowledge when you are inspired by something.

D2W Character Scenario

When Greg read the flyer for the youth entrepreneurial program he was really interested and signed up the first day. The program was designed to teach basic business knowledge, and coupled with his desire and interest in being a businessman like his dad, he was well on his way to proving he was serious. Greg learned so much from the 12-week youth entrepreneurial program. He framed his certificate in his room and started working on his business plan.

Skills

What can you do? Are you good with your hands? Do you like taking things apart and putting them back together? What about drawing? I remember my cousin used to draw airplanes and cars when he was younger, and now as an adult, his art has matured into creating mosaic designs with colorful tiles. He loved drawing and could do it for hours. What about you? What are you good at? Are you a good writer? Do you love creating stories? You might become an author or maybe a movie script writer. What about your mathematical skills? Believe it or not some people love math. They like the mental work of figuring out the problems. These skills are essential for careers such as an engineer, scientist, and architect. Your interests normally dictate what skills you are interested in developing. **Skills are defined as the ability to do something well, arising from talent, training, or practice.** Skills are the things you can do well. As a young person, you may not have a lot of skills to list on your resume, but your job is to develop your interests and build employable skills.

Do you believe that, as an adult, you will have to use the skills you are learning in school? When you are in school, you are focused on developing academic skills. English, Math, and Science classes build the necessary foundational skills you need to be competent even with everyday tasks. You will need good comprehension skills to read and understand complicated legal documents. I have written business letters and even had to recall how to do algebraic formulas from my Algebra and Chemistry classes to analyze financial problems at work.

Think about how difficult your life would be if you could not read. Life would definitely be harder without that skill. You would have to depend on others or get special software to help you comprehend what you read. When I was growing up, we had typing classes in high school. It was essential to learn how to type, even for the guys. With the new touch computers and the voice-activated software, you might not know how to type outside of 'texting with a few fingers,' but it used to be a big deal to pass a typing test of 55 words per minute or higher for an administrative job. At my first adult job, I had to pass a test for Microsoft Word and Excel to get hired as a secretary making about $14 per hour. When you are looking for a job, you will have to demonstrate you have certain skills. These skills should be listed on your resume. You definitely want to have an impressive array of skills. There will always be a line of other people just as qualified and skilled to do the job you want. You must be competent and competitive. This means you have to stay committed to building your skills continually.

D2W Character Scenario

Eliza joined the Journalism Club at her school. She had worked herself up from a researcher to a journalist and now she was the lead editor and traveled to several community events for journalism assignments. She was gifted at writing and was very interested in meeting new people and visiting places she had never been. It gave her a chance to escape the pressures and boredom at home. While her brothers and sisters stayed at home on the weekends doing nothing, Eliza was traveling with her journalism team going to weekend events, interviewing community leaders, and filming their events with her camera crew. This was fun. She was becoming a serious reporter. Her teachers always said she could have a career in news reporting and journalism. Her written and verbal communication was excellent. She wondered if this would be something she would do as a career. Maybe she was good enough.

Experiences

What have you experienced? Have you volunteered in your community? Are your experiences worth listing on your resume? Did you participate on a soccer team? Have you volunteered and traveled to orphanages in another country? Have you interned for an organization? It is so important to enrich your life with quality experiences. Having valuable experiences stretches you as a person and gives you more options and choices to choose from. **Experiences are defined as the knowledge gained from what one has observed, encountered, or undergone.** Pretend you have traveled around the world. You have been to Europe, Africa, and Australia. You speak French, Spanish, and even Japanese fluently.

You have met great people and maintain relationships by emailing and visiting friends from all these countries you have visited. Your interest in Art and Music has afforded you chances to be in music concerts, theater productions, and art competitions. Your most prized accomplishment is your recent music CD release. As a teenager, you have worked a few part-time jobs. You have worked as an intern at your mother's dentist office. If these were your experiences, people would be shocked you have been exposed to so many opportunities as a young person. People who are traveled extensively are more cultivated because they have been exposed to different cultures and people. The more experiences you have, the more options and areas of interests you can draw from.

All of us have had experiences, whether positive or negative. Make it your mission to seek out experiences that you can learn from. Seek out internships and volunteer opportunities that can point you toward a successful career. Positive and rewarding experiences when you are younger can be a stepping stone for your next series of opportunities. Even negative experiences provide knowledge of what not to do and the opportunity to build strong character. *"Sometimes the only way to ever find yourself is to get completely lost." (Kellie Elmore)* Life is about discovery. We can find purpose as we open our lives to new experiences. Our lives are formed one experience at a time. The goal in life is to let every experience prepare you for your future.

D2W Character Scenario

Michael was nervous at his job interview. How would he explain being fired from his Bucky Burgers job? He had to admit that he was immature and took his first job for granted. This new job was important to him because it would provide direct skills for a career in the information technology industry. He had his resume and practiced interview questions for weeks. His mentors provided letters of recommendations. In the interview he shared his experiences from his first job as a cashier at Bucky Burgers and talked about how he learned about teamwork and being dependable. The interviewer must have thought he really learned his lesson because Michael got the job. Michael called his best friend Greg to tell him the news.

See how the D2W character Michael's previous knowledge, skills, and experiences prepared him for his next opportunities. You have to commit to the 'Highways of Learning' and build your life. Time is ticking. Employers expect to see a resume that shows you have been busy building your knowledge, skills, and experiences continually. They do not want to see a lot of gaps of inactivity in your life. It would be similar to a GPS tracking

your every movement and then all of a sudden you go off the road. When you are sedentary and not making efforts to learn and pursue your dreams and goals, you are being unproductive. You are off the road. Do not let this happen to you. Employers will ask you what you were doing with your time. All of your learning is the foundation for the next years. Do not lose momentum. Keep moving forward.

D2W Stop Sign Alert

If you want to advance in life, you must be committed to being a life learner. Learning does not happen only in the classroom and doesn't stop when school is over. Learning takes place in many ways and should be a continual process. Make sure your learning process is not just to make a good grade. Stay involved and active in learning throughout your life.

D2W Assignment: It's Your Turn

Fill out the basic information to start your resume. Provide a brief statement describing yourself. List your school experience and academic accomplishments. List some skills you have obtained. Detail any work experiences. List any school clubs, leadership positions, and volunteer experiences you are involved in.

RESUME

Personal Description:

I am diligent and dependable. I am a serious student with a 3.5 grade point average.

I am enthusiastic and dedicated and involved in sports and leadership roles at my school.

I am a teamplayer and have great communication skills.

Fill in information for your resume.

_____

_____

KNOWLEDGE

Fill in information for your resume.

What are your educational achievements?

3.5-grade point average

Honors student

_____

_____

_____

SKILLS

What work skills do you have?

Work Skills and Abilities:

Galaxy Movie Theatre – Team leader

Bucky Burgers – Cash Register

Strong computer skills

Articulate/Good communicator

Strong math and writing skills

_____

_____

_____

_____

EXPERIENCE

What leadership, school clubs, community clubs, and volunteer experiences do you have?

School/Community Experiences:

Captain of the Football Team

Volunteered at Concerned Youth Council

Volunteered at Neighborhood Clean-up Project

Youth YMCA Summer Camp Leader

_____

_____

_____

_____

Lesson 4: Ten Golden Rules of the Road

When we talk about rules we are dealing with the best principles, attitudes, and belief systems that help us live our lives in the best possible way. The rules we are focusing on are success principles. People change, but principles usually do not change. Principles of life are true no matter what the focus area. One of my most cherished motivational speakers is the late Miles Monroe. In one of his books, I remember him sharing, *"If you do not know the purpose of a thing it will destroy you."* Being destroyed could simply mean not existing any longer or losing instead of winning in life. We need to know the purpose of rules and respect them. *What is the purpose of rules? Are they designed to block us from having fun and enjoying life?* Rules simply protect us. Nobody is trying to limit your fun. There are 10 Golden Rules of the Road. They are: **1) Ownership, 2) Self-Esteem, 3) Expectations, 4) Motivation, 5) Success versus Failure, 6) Performance, 7) Rewards, 8) Mentors, 9) Accountability, and 10) Self-Evaluation.** If we learn the rules, we will have a greater understanding how to live successful lives.

Rule 1: Ownership - *Drive in Your Own Lane*

You might have heard this word before. You probably can figure out the meaning when someone says, "You must take ownership for your life." Basically, this means you are responsible for your own life. You might as well not blame others for your actions and decisions. If you are D2W, then you "drive in your own lane." Whether it is getting your homework done on time, cleaning up your room, or even something as important as getting to your part-time job on time, you cannot give away your responsibilities or expect someone else to do them for you. **Ownership is the responsible action to take control for your life, attitude, and decisions.** This does not mean you cannot get advice or help from others. It simply means you understand it is your responsibility to get things done for your life. For example, if you are sick from school and you missed several important Geometry assignments, who's responsibility is it to get the notes, schedule time with the teacher, and ensure your grade will not suffer? When your grade is lowered from a B to a C because you were not responsible, do you blame the teacher?

You really have to "own" who you are and what your life is about. Nobody gets to lead or define your life once you are an adult. That is your responsibility. You must be fully aware of your responsibilities and the consequences that will result if you do not meet them. This goes hand in hand with Maturity Test #1: Identifying and Meeting Your Responsibilities, as we discussed earlier. We should not let other people rob us of this maturing role. Nobody who really respects you as your own person wants to cripple and rob you of your ownership. People that care for you want you to be your best. <u>Your best is having the capacity to learn who you are, make mistakes, and grow from your experiences.</u>

Sometimes you might be tempted to let parents and guardians do things that you can do for yourself. As you mature, you can be proud of yourself when you "take ownership" of your life and make the right decisions. You have the privilege of taking control of your life and responding appropriately. You have the right to own the 'pink slip' for your life decisions and be responsible for the necessary 'repairs and maintenance' to keep your life on track. This is how you learn and grow. This is how you win in life.

D2W Character Scenario

When it came to 'smarts,' Antonio was the envy of everyone. He was always the smartest student in the classroom. He even was voted in his high school as the 'Most Likely to Succeed.' From a young age, he had desired to be a pediatrician. He hoped to be the first one in his family to finish college. Others had started college in his family, but never finished. When his counselor gave his graduating class a list of scholarships, he did not waste any time preparing his scholarship applications. He could not put the cost of his college on his family. He had to take responsibility if he wanted to make his dream a reality.

D2W Assignment: It's Your Turn

What areas of your life do you need to take more responsibility of and not wait on others to remind you of what you should be doing?

Areas of Responsibility	What will you do today to be responsible?
1. _____	_____
2. _____	_____
3. _____	_____

Rule 2: Self-Esteem – *What is your price tag?*

We have heard this word kicked around a lot. What is healthy self-esteem? **Self-esteem is the worth or value you give yourself as a person.** If I esteem something, that means I consider it worthy. I believe it has value. It is worth my attention, my best efforts, and my money. Do you believe this about yourself? Is your life worth the effort of pursuing your dreams?

We esteem others all the time. We go the extra mile for friends. Even if we do not feel like it, we show up because we care for them. Do we do this for ourselves? It makes sense that, if you are going to consider other people and other things worth your effort, you definitely should be your own best friend. If anybody is going to say nice things about you or want you to succeed, then you should be the first person to believe in yourself. *"I believe in you. I know you have what it takes. You are going to be great."* Are these the messages you tell yourself? *"I am worth it. I am worth the money. I am worth the effort. My dreams and goals matter."* Most people do not verbally say these positive messages to themselves. They will say them openly about their family members, friends, even acquaintances, but they do not believe or treat themselves with the same love and respect. We judge ourselves so harshly at times. We know all about our personal challenges and failures. Regardless, like the others we love, we need to have unconditional love for ourselves, which does not change whether we succeed or fail.

If you were interested in football and wanted to go to an expensive summer camp that costs $800 dollars, would you pay for yourself to go if you had the money? Are you worth that kind of investment? You might ask your parents to shovel over that kind of money, but if you earned the money from a part-time job, would you pay for yourself to go? When we invest in our own personal development it indicates we believe in our potential. We demonstrate to ourselves that we are worth the investment. In fact, many investors want to see how much effort and money you have invested in your dream first before they will. You have to demonstrate a commitment to yourself before others will. The only way you will make a real commitment toward your dreams is if you have healthy self-esteem and believe you are worthy.

D2W Character Scenario

Melanie was unsure if she really should go after the head cheerleader position. She was talented and had experience with dance choreography from her 10 years in the dance academy. She did not believe she was as popular and pretty as the other girls that wanted the position. Her boyfriend Michael kept assuring her that she was just as talented and she should try out if she really wanted it. Melanie was shocked when the Head Cheerleader Director called her back for a second audition. Maybe she was good enough. She began to believe that she had just as much chance as anyone else.

D2W Assignment: It's Your Turn

List three qualities you like about yourself below. Ask three different groups (parents, friends, and teachers) what your best qualities are. Write down the responses and determine if there are any similarities.

My best qualities are:	Parents/Guardians	Friends	Teachers
1. _____	_____	_____	_____
2. _____	_____	_____	_____
3. _____	_____	_____	_____

Are there any similarities or differences in the responses? What did you learn about what others believe about you?

_____

_____

Rule 3: Expectations - *How far can you go?*

When you are walking across the stage at your high school graduation, what do you expect out of your life? Do you expect to receive a college degree? What job or career do you expect to have? Do you expect to have a lifestyle where you can afford to travel to several different countries or struggle with basic expenses? If you are involved in sports or other extracurricular competitive activities, do you expect to qualify for state or national championships? **Expectation is what you believe you are capable of achieving and what you want to receive in your life.** What do you expect to achieve with your life? Get very clear about the expectations you have for your life. Realize what you are telling yourself on the inside and believing about yourself. **What you expect, you will prepare for.** If I expect that I am a good candidate for a job and I am competitive, then I will prepare for the interview and expect good results. I expect to achieve. If you are not your own best cheerleader, then it is time to stop and get this rule working for you. If you do not believe you are capable of achieving your dreams, who will believe for you? This is a huge determinant of success. The expectations you have for yourself make the difference between whether you will quit and give up or keep plugging away until you get what you want.

I expect great things out of my life. What do you expect of yourself? When you graduate from high school, there are usually two students recognized for their excellent academic performance. These two recognitions are the valedictorian and the salutatorian. These are coveted positions because these students are recognized for having the most impressive academic life. There are other titles such as "Best Dressed" or "Most Likely to Succeed" for high school seniors. These titles are simply a way for others to express what they perceive or expect out of your life. **Have you ever asked your parents or guardians what they expect out of your life?** What about your best friends? Ask them what they expect you will do with your life in the next 3, 5, 10, and 15 years. This will be an enlightening assignment because you get to be in the 'front seat' and learn what others expect from your life. Their positive expectations can really motivate you to do your best.

It is good to know what the most important, caring people in your life believe about you. I said caring because not everyone treats us with respect or care. Not everyone believes the greatest things about you. *"You will never amount to anything." You are just like your ....* *(fill in the blank).* Some people have grown up with these negative words spoken over their lives, unfortunately. These hurtful and irresponsible words are expectations from either hurt or unloving people. Any words or expectations remotely similar to the sting of these words have to be erased and rejected from your memory. I hope you never heard any hurtful words like these. Regardless though, you MUST rise above any negative expectations and do the complete opposite. **EXPECT great things for yourself.**

You first believe, and then you receive. **You cannot rise higher than your expectations. If you say you cannot, you cannot. I ask again, what do you expect of yourself?** What you believe about yourself is CRITICAL. This can be a strong driving force you can use to accomplish great things. All negative beliefs MUST be erased. Remember, it all starts in the mind. What you imagine in your mind is what you bring to life. What do you see out of the windshield for your life? **Imagining or visualizing your way forward is how you win in life.** That is why it is so important for you to focus on positive thoughts. Regardless of what is going on in your life, you have to force yourself to believe in something better in the future. You have to create the positive energy in your mind to change your life. You can start by imagining what you are going to accomplish in this school year. If you are on the basketball team, it might be the visual images of you making the winning shot at your basketball game. Whatever you are involved in, you simply start imagining and expecting yourself to achieve. **Greatness starts with what you expect for yourself.**

What are you expecting of your life?

Subject	*My Expectations*
Finding good friends	*I expect to have trusting and fun friendships.*
School Success	*I expect to make the Honor Roll this year.*
Financial life	*I expect to open a bank account and save money.*
Health & Fitness	*I expect to exercise, eat healthy, and maintain a healthy weight.*

Speak positive words to yourself. Stop all negative messages. Do not think them. Do not speak them. When you have a negative thought, reject it immediately and say out loud "I reject that thought." Immediately say something great about your life. I am serious. Face yourself in the mirror and say to yourself, *"I believe in you. I expect greatness from you."* These are the words and thoughts of a person committed to success. Speak these words out loud to yourself. Your ears need to hear your voice. Do not be shy. You are building your expectations of yourself. If you are really bold, let your parents and friends hear you say these words about yourself. Echo these words to other important people and let them know you expect great things out of their lives also. Never underestimate the power of the spoken word. This is how you build your life and live the life of a winner. You deserve great things in life. You are designed and destined to win. Believe it. Expect it.

D2W Character Scenario

Eliza finished the internship application and submitted it to her career counselor. She really wanted to get the nomination for the Mayor's Youth Leadership Internship, but she did not want to get her hopes up. This was a competitive internship. It would look very impressive to colleges. As she submitted her application and picked up her school bag to leave the counseling office, Ms. Clark, the career counselor said, "Good luck. I really hope you do well." Eliza mistakenly let out a sigh and said, "That would be a miracle." Ms. Clark stopped her and asked her why she had such a lack of confidence. Eliza shared with her that after failing to get recognized for the last two internships, she did not expect to do well. After Ms. Clark talked to Eliza, she slowly started changing her attitude and got over the previously failed experiences. She started believing things would change and she would soon be rewarded for all her hard work. When Ms. Clark called her into the office two weeks later to announce she got the internship, Eliza was so excited and thanked Ms. Clark for helping her to develop a winning attitude.

D2W Assignment: It's Your Turn

List three things you are working on currently. Write down the topic or area. Finish the "I expect" statement. List the actions you are taking to be successful.

I am working on…	I expect….	My actions are…
1. _____	_____	_____
2. _____	_____	_____
3. _____	_____	_____

Rule 4: Motivation - *What makes you go?*

We all want to accomplish great things, but sometimes we do not feel like making an effort. I believe we have all experienced times when we were desperately trying to make ourselves do things we really did not feel like doing. Whether it is completing a term paper for your English class, completing a lap around the track for P.E. class, or raking the leaves in your backyard, we all know it is not easy to get ourselves in the mood to complete tasks that are not exciting to us. How do we motivate ourselves to do things that we know is beneficial to us? How do we stay focused?

Motivation is defined as the reason why you do what you do. We can find the answer by looking at the root word 'motive.' The definition of 'motive' is the reason or purpose for doing something. It is easier to be motivated when your reason is big enough. If the pleasure that will come as a result of your effort is worth it, then you can use that to get you focused. What if you were a wrestler and had six weeks to put on 10lbs to enter a new weight class to qualify for state championships. You have to remind yourself how it will feel to qualify. Is the prize big enough to move you to do the work and get off the couch?

Think about the outcomes of your decisions. Be a person that focuses on the outcomes. It really boils down to just that. Consider whether the task is important for what you want to accomplish. Are you willing to face the consequences of not doing the task? Which outcome do you want to experience: Finish the task and reap the rewards or slack off and face the consequences? Do you spend the next hour watching television or do you read the novel your English teacher assigned to be prepared for class tomorrow? If you want to stay motivated, remind yourself of the prize or the outcome. What will you get for your hard work? Is it worth your best effort? **If your "reason" or your "why" is big enough, then it will be the motivator to help you do the work.** Your efforts at anything in life are worth it if the outcome is worth it. **Visualize yourself attaining the prize to motivate you toward action.**

What else can help you? This is where your character comes in. You have to build your character so that, when you are faced with these moments, you will have the discipline and determination to stay motivated and make the right choices. The mental effort to start the work is the most difficult, but once you begin focusing on accomplishing your task, it gets easier to stay  focused. Every time we overcome complacency and laziness, we gain the discipline to motivate ourselves when harder choices come. If you can stay motivated to do your homework daily, then you should be able to motivate yourself for other things. It takes the same determination.

D2W Character Scenario

It was early Saturday morning, and the last thing Antonio wanted to do was to get up and go running with his new trainer on the weekend. He was tired from studying for his History test the night before. He and Janice had committed to taking their health seriously, and they had hired a fitness trainer to really get into shape. He felt like calling and saying he was too tired, but he thought of how this might influence Janice to slack off on her weight loss goals. He visualized asking Eliza to the prom and shopping for his tuxedo suit. Losing 20lbs would really be great. He pushed his feelings to the side, rolled out of bed, and called Janice to say he would pick her up.

D2W Assignment: It's Your Turn

Identify three tasks that you know you have to do, but you do not feel like doing. List what you will do to motivate yourself to accomplish them. Identify what the reward and consequence will be for each task.

Tasks	Things you will do to motivate yourself	Reward/Consequence
1. _____	_____	_____
2. _____	_____	_____
3. _____	_____	_____

Rule 5: Success vs. Failure - *Drive Past the Bumps*

It is so crucial to understand this rule. We all want to be successful, but we have to face some failures. If you do not understand how to handle failures, you could spiral into discouragement when your life does not go as planned. **Success vs. Failure is the assessment you give an experience when you attempt something, and it turns out right or wrong in your estimation.** I believe success and failure are two sides of the same coin. It depends on what side you are looking at. It is not if you fail, but when you fail. This is something you have to get comfortable with. I am not saying you should want to fail --- that is not the goal, but if you do not try things because you are too afraid to fail or you get so overwhelmed and depressed when you are not perfect at something, that mindset is a bigger failure than the situation. Whether it is a grade on an English test or your performance at your dance recital, failure does not have to be final if you can find the silver lining, as they say.

Let us diagnose failure because many people get tripped up by this, including me. **What is happening when we fail?** Whether those experiences are related to school classes, sporting activities, or relationships, failure is just "a failed attempt." If we make a D on a Geometry test and go over the problems, we did not know, basically we are going to discover the information that we have not mastered. Failure moves you forward if you learn and recognize what does not work and you improve your approach. We become aware of what we do not know. It does not mean that life is over. It does not mean that success is unattainable. It simply means we have more to learn. We have to journey toward another place on the map to achieve what we want. The trick is to not get stuck in a failed experience where you are ashamed and discouraged from moving ahead. Failure can serve our purpose to bring us closer to where we want to go.

If you visualize a road, see your successes and failures as points on your road. Do not make failure and success more than it is. Failure is just a point on the road indicating where we are and success happens to be another point on the road where we want to go.
If we can see failure as an opportunity illuminating the path toward progress, then we can mentally get over the trauma of the failed experience. I know it is not easy to move beyond failure seconds after you fail, but with time and with the right mindset, failed experiences will be in the "rearview mirror" and a distant memory.

We have talked about failure. Let's talk about success. If you won a national chess competition a year ago, you could not "hang your hat" on that single success for the rest of your life. Some people do that. They reduce their life to a single experience. They win at something, and they talk about it forever. They measure and define the rest of their lives by that one successful experience. There are other successes to be achieved. I am not saying this so you cannot enjoy your hard-earned success or feel proud when you receive your trophies, but do not make it the foundation of your life. Success is to be enjoyed and rewarded, but be careful not to make a few successes support your whole life.

You might have great successes when it comes to your education, but be an absolute failure at relationships. You cannot get along with parents, friends, and you have trouble maintaining a healthy relationship with a girlfriend or boyfriend. It is important to be successful in relationships also. Stop talking about all the A's and B's you got on your report card without dealing with your unhealthy lifestyle and weight issues. Success in life is measured in several areas. Let me give you another example to show you what I am speaking about. There is always an athlete from high school that had all the girls and talent scouts drooling, but when he is all grown up and his high school years are over, where is his success? If he is still bragging about how he scored the winning touchdown in his high school senior year 20 years ago and does not have any new successes to talk about, is he still successful? Yesterday's successes are not enough to hold you up for a lifetime.

All of life is about making progress in all areas, not just one or two and not just for one moment of your life. At the end of the day, sometimes we fail, and sometimes we win.
Do yourself a favor. Gain some perspective. When you fail, or do not achieve something you

put effort toward, find the rainbow in your circumstances. Do not let one experience color your world forever. You are more than one experience, whether it was a success or failure.

Learn and obey this rule now while you are young. Remember successes and failures are just singular points on the road of your life to learn from. There are adults right now who have remained trapped in their own minds and cannot move to their next level because of past successes and failures. Escape this trap. *"Success is measured not so much by the position that one has reached in life as by the obstacles which he has overcome while trying to succeed." (Booker T. Washington)* Keep moving toward your next adventures instead of being stuck in the past. When you work hard at something, focus on your progress, not just the failures or successes. *"I am not what happened to me, I am what I choose to become." (C.G. Jung)*

D2W Character Scenario

Every time the football game came on television Michael's older brother started talking about how great he was on the football field in his college days. He only played for two years in college and quit. He was expecting his first child with his girlfriend, and the pressures of starting a family made him quit school and get serious about his job. He was depressed about not living up to his dream. Michael did not want to end up like that. His success on the football field in high school was impressive. All the college scouts came to his games and always talked about his college career. Michael had plans to make it all the way to the NFL. He knew that if he quit and did not work hard, he would never make it. His coach let him know that his chance for a football career was not factored on a few losses or wins on the football field, but his overall performance. He encouraged him to focus on building his skills and the mental stamina and determination needed to accomplish his dreams.

D2W Assignment: It's Your Turn

List three of your successes and failures. Identify what you have learned about yourself and how you can use these experiences for your next achievements.

Successes	Failures	How can you use these experiences?
1. _____	_____	_____
2. _____	_____	_____
3. _____	_____	_____

Rule 6: Performance - *Are We There Yet?*

What are you involved in? Sports? ASB school club? Yearbook? It is important for you to be active and involved. I did not say busy. The goal is not for you to stay busy so you will not get into trouble. I have heard parents say they want their kids to stay busy with the hope that they will not get in trouble. That is not the goal. The higher aim is to be involved in activities that will further personal growth. Being a more caring, competent, and competitive person is the goal.

If you are involved in competitive sports, your goal is to perform well and win. **Win the trophy. Win the championship.** To do this, you have to perform. *Are We There Yet?* **Performance is what you accomplish compared to what you want to accomplish.** Have you crossed the finish line? **Set the goal. Train hard. Get the gold.** Competitive sports and other competitive opportunities help give you a sense of pride in your accomplishments.

Every young person needs to be exposed to the conditions of competition in some capacity. In life, you will meet people who excel on your level and others that exceed your talents. If you run track, there will be faster runners. If you play baseball or softball, there will be hitters that can hit farther than you. That is okay. When you meet up with other people who have superior talents, study them, and see what they do to be great. Meanwhile, perfect your gift and talents and perform in whatever you are passionate about. Get to your highest level.

Prepare to be your best. No point in getting upset, jealous, or feeling that you are not good enough compared to others. You need to know how to deal with competition. Winners do not shrink down in the midst of greatness. They rise to the occasion. Winners study their opponents, learn what they can, and incorporate what they have learned to increase their own performance.

You will meet up with competition all your life. You may not be in competitive sports, but when you are going after an internship or a job, a lead part in the play, a scholarship, you are competing. Your knowledge, skills, and experiences are being compared to the other candidates or applicants. This is why you cannot lower the hurdle for your life. You cannot coast through life, not finish your college education, or fail to get yourself prepared to compete for career and business opportunities. Others are preparing themselves to compete, so you must stay focused.

I have talked a lot about competition because it is a part of life. There is a time for external competitors; however, winning in life is really about competing with yourself. Life is mostly about measuring up to the personal vision you have for yourself. Your performance is based on what you expect for your life. Remember the Golden Rule on Expectations? We are talking about performing against the blueprint of our own destiny. *Are We There Yet?* Are you on track and performing at the peak of your abilities? Your performance is the output of your successes and failures. It is about measurement. You either pass the test, or you do not. You either make the varsity basketball team, or you do not. **When you succeed or fail, you evaluate your performance, but you do not lower your standards or lose confidence in yourself.** You have to be honest with yourself. You perform well when you prepare well. It is about your diligent efforts. Be proud of yourself when you work hard at something. Even if you are not crowned the winner, you are a winner based on the personal progress you make. That is gold in itself. **Be D2W.**

D2W Character Scenario

Greg was so proud of himself for investing his first $500 in his Young Millionaire's Investment Club he started. He diligently reviewed his investment account every week and realized his initial investment had grown to $900 in his first 6 months. He had set a goal to grow his portfolio to $1,500 before the end of the year. He was on track and had six more months to go. He could not wait until he told Michael, his best friend, about his progress.

D2W Assignment: It's Your Turn

Rewrite your three expectations from Rule 3. Identify what you achieved and how you feel about your performance. Tell three people about your accomplishments. Use this statement: "I am proud of myself. I have achieved… (fill in the blank)." Share how you felt about your performance using those specific words.

Expectations	How did you perform?	Who did you tell?
1. _____	_____	_____
2. _____	_____	_____
3. _____	_____	_____

How did it make you feel to speak about yourself?

_____

_____

Rule 7: Rewards - *What do you get for your effort?*

For every accomplishment, there should be a visible reward, benefit, or at least something valuable, even if it is only a compliment or verbal acknowledgment. When you are recognized for your achievements, I call it a 'Stage of Recognition.' Just as if you were on stage singing or dancing and people applauded you for your performance—that is what a 'Stage of Recognition' is. It is your time to take your bows. Everyone needs their moment where they shine and have a stage where they can be recognized and rewarded.

Rewards are the prizes and good things you get in life for your hard work. If you have a part-time job and you work for two weeks, you get a paycheck, which is a direct result and benefit of your efforts. The tangible benefit is money. You work; you get rewarded. This is your incentive for working. It is a transaction. You give; you receive. It is not always about money, though. The reward for volunteering is experience. The reward for good character and perseverance is success. **Do the work. The reward will come.**

What do I get for my efforts? What rewards have you received? Have you received trophies, awards, or certificates for what you have accomplished? Recognition or rewards for your achievements are important. They reinforce your commitment and efforts. Place your certificates, awards, and trophies so they are visible. When you receive your high school diploma, college diploma, and certificates they serve as tangible reminders to validate your achievements and hard work. **The rewards need to be worth the effort.** Sometimes you will get a visible reward. Sometimes you will receive verbal recognition. However, in case nobody acknowledges you, learn to be your own cheerleader! You do not have to wait on others. Congratulate yourself. Be proud of yourself! No need to brag. You know when you have put real effort toward your goals. Remember to give others their "props" when they deserve it. People need to know and hear that you are proud of them. You need this too. Achievement brings rewards. Keep striving. Life knows how to support and recognize your efforts.

D2W Character Scenario

Eliza was on the stage with all the other students receiving the Mayor's Youth Leadership Award for the Year. She had worked really hard to get here. She was nervous right before her name was called. She had entitled her speech 'Making an Impact in Your Community.' Her submittal had netted her a $1,000 scholarship. All her hard work was worth it. She also learned she was awarded the competitive internship for the Mayor's youth journalist position. Her parents were so proud of her. She could see them smiling on the front row with her younger sister and brother.

D2W Assignment: It's Your Turn

Write down three of your achievements and the rewards (trophies, certificates, scholarships, money, acknowledgments, etc.) you received for your hard work. How did you feel when you were recognized? Identify if the effort was worth the reward. Answer what normally motivates you to give your best effort.

Achievement / Rewards	How did it make you feel?	Worth it? (Y or N)
1. _____	_____	_____
2. _____	_____	_____
3. _____	_____	_____

What motivates you to give your best effort?

_____

_____

Rule 8: Mentors - *Stop reinventing the wheel*

Who do you know that encourages you to do your best and expects great things from you? Do you have these important people in your life? These people are called mentors.

Mentors are people that direct you toward progress, inspire you, and share life lessons to help avoid costly mistakes. You need living, breathing examples that can inspire and motivate you to do your best in life. Whether it is an

accomplished person in a career industry you are interested in or a person who simply encourages your personal growth, it is essential that you have positive examples of people who believe in you. **Mentors are people along your path. Mentors are like landmarks or road signs.** They point the way forward. They guide and give you direction. Mentors are not only for academic, career, or business pursuits, but also personal development. Your mentors could be your parents or guardians. Mentors could be a teacher or pastor that has taken time with you. This special person could be a track or football coach.

Many times, mentors are adults, but it could be a person in college or slightly older than you. It could be an older sister or brother you look up to. Build a mentoring relationship with older college students, business and community leaders, or senior citizens with great life experiences. When people around you seem to interest and intrigue you, they possibly could serve as mentors. No matter the individual, mentors encourage you toward personal success. You should have mentors that can share their career or business experiences especially if you are interested in similar professional areas. They probably can help you find internships and future jobs. Your mentors may serve as a reference on your college submissions or job applications. They can write letters of recommendation for you. Even if they do not have the answers from personal experience, they usually go out of their way to connect you to the resources and information you need.

Many youth organizations assist with finding mentors. Take advantage of these opportunities. However, do not wait for others to seek you out. Be proactive and find mentors on your own. Learn about their journey. Learn about their successes and the challenges they overcame when they were younger. People who take the time to mentor youth are usually passionate people who are willing to share their life experiences. They probably have special people that made a big difference in their lives. Of course, always include your parents or guardians by letting them know who you are interested in as a mentor.

Important note: After you have started a mentoring relationship, make sure you show your mentors how much you value them. Send them thank you cards. These important relationships need to be managed and could last even into your adulthood. *"No man is an island to himself" (John Donne).* You cannot succeed alone. Ask anyone who is truly successful. If you are wise, you will learn all you can from your mentors. They will serve as a great asset and challenge you toward greatness. You should respect them because they have personal successes and they faced the challenges that you can learn from.

Rule 9: Accountability –*Who's watching your blind spots?*

When you take the time to develop relationships with important people and share your goals with them, something dynamic happens to help you stay focused. You feel compelled to accomplish what you said you would do. You become accountable to them. The word 'accountable' is not a word or concept that we usually use in our daily lives. If you were talking about finances, you might give an 'account' of where your money was going. Well, what about your dreams and goals? Who are the people you share or give 'account' to concerning your dreams and goals? Who cares enough to follow your personal growth and challenge you on what you said you would accomplish? Doesn't this sound like the role of a mentor? **Accountability is voluntarily listening and giving account to trustworthy people who care about your progress.** *Who's watching your blind spots?* Being accountable is not a bad thing, but a helpful opportunity where other people are concerned about your personal success.

For example, if you shared with your dance teacher that you were going to try out for the spring dance competition and you did not, then when you saw her she might ask you how your audition went. If you were saving money to buy your first car, your friend might ask how much money you had saved. If your grandmother always bragged about how smart you were at family gatherings and gave you money for your grades,  you probably would find it difficult to let her know you flunked a grade or did not graduate. See what I mean about being accountable?

All of us need trustworthy people in our lives who expect great things from us. I use the word trustworthy because they encourage us, not shame us. Their words build our confidence and do not tear us down. We only become accountable to people we can trust with our dreams. These are people who will not let us walk away from our dreams without a fight. Even when we experience failure, they still believe in our greatness and remind us of our self-worth. We share our dreams and goals with them and do not want to disappoint them. We update them on our personal progress. They hold us "accountable" to our commitments and expect us to live to our fullest potential. They push us to be greater than we are. They are invaluable because they challenge us to be our best and watch our lives with great expectation.

D2W Character Scenario

Janice, Eliza, and Michael understood the importance of appreciating the people in their lives who believed in their dreams. Janice could not give up on her passion for ballet after her mentor encouraged her to pursue her dreams. Eliza was so thankful for her counselor encouraging her to apply for the internship. Michael had to keep his grades up. He would be devastated if he was placed on academic probation and could not play in the upcoming state football championship game especially since the new football coach spent several weeks training him for the running back position.

D2W Assignment: It's Your Turn

Write down the people you are accountable to. These might be the same people you listed as mentors. Ask them what they believe and expect from your life.

Accountable People   What do they believe and expect from your life?

1. _____   _____

2. _____   _____

3. _____   _____

Rule 10: Self-Evaluation – *Check Your Controls*

Self-evaluation is the key to continuing your progress toward any goal.

Self-evaluation is an honest estimation of how you are performing. It helps you to gain an understanding of what areas to focus on for progress. Where are you on the road? Are you closer to your destination?

Check your controls. Self-evaluation deals with checking your controls, which means you need to

be honest with yourself. You cannot hide from your performance. Some people do not want to be aware of how they are doing, especially if they are failing in some areas. However, you cannot have this attitude in life if you want to succeed. We are not always on track with our goals. You cannot continue to make progress if you are too scared to face the truth and unwilling to evaluate yourself. **All successful people monitor their lives and evaluate whether they are accomplishing the goals they have set for themselves.**

For example, if you were a wrestler or a ballerina and you videotaped your performance, could you watch yourself to see what you did right or wrong? If you needed a high grade on your History essay to get off of academic probation and you rushed through your homework to go to the movies with friends, would you be honest about your performance when you received a low grade for unsatisfactory work? Would you evaluate your decisions and your level of effort? It is not always easy to face your failures and stay positive enough to work on the areas you need to improve. I remember when I was in speech competition in high school and college. Sometimes we had to videotape our performances to prepare for the next competition. I was always so nervous to be taped. I was critical when I messed up or tripped over my words. I also was uncomfortable when I had to read my evaluations from the judges. Eventually, I got over being self-conscious and started to use this information to get better. Self-evaluation helped me to win several championships. This is how winners do it. They are not afraid of self-evaluation because they understand the purpose is to help improve performance, not to be critical. All athletes have to judge themselves. All scholars have to evaluate themselves. When you receive your school grades, your academic performance is being evaluated by your teachers. Your academic report cards are the outcome or the result of your performance.

Self-evaluation is a rule that you impose on yourself. You demonstrate you are mature when you can review your work and take any necessary steps to improve your performance. Be proactive and do not wait for others to judge your work. Successful people do what it takes to get to the next level. Successful people seek information and feedback instead of avoiding it. They use this information for personal evaluation. It is not about criticizing, but evaluating your work. Be true to where you are and make plans to keep moving forward. **Be D2W.**

D2W Character Scenario

Melanie did it to herself again. She put so much effort into cheerleading after school that she did not focus on finishing the online classes her counselor set up for her. Her counselor warned her that, if she did not make up her credits from her failed courses, she might have to attend summer school. She would not be in this mess if she had made a serious effort and not hung out with Michael and her friends after school. Now she had to cancel her travel plans with friends. It was time to get serious and do the hard work.

D2W Assignment: It's Your Turn

Rewrite three of your dreams or some of your responsibilities. (Refer back to lesson 1 or chapter 3.) Rate your effort. (1 being lowest; 5 being highest) Identify if you are on track. What else can you do to improve your outcomes?

	Dreams/Goals	Efforts? (1-5)	On Track? (Y or N)	Improvements
1.	_____	_____	_____	_____
2.	_____	_____	_____	_____
3.	_____	_____	_____	_____

D2W Stop Sign Alert

There are principles or rules on how to live a better life. Figure out the purpose of the rules and value them. Do not despise them. You will be more successful when you respect and follow the rules in life.

Lesson 5: 4D's on a Destructive Road

There is a road that is not to be traveled on. It is a destructive road. There are four stages on this road, which increasingly gets worse and takes you further away from your dreams and goals. Unfortunately, all of us find ourselves on this road at various times in our lives because of our humanity. **These four stages are 1) distractions, 2) delays, 3) detours, and 4) dead ends**. If you can recognize quickly when you are about to drive on a destructive road, then you might be able to steer clear of it. If you look up and you realize you are on a destructive road, you need to navigate and maneuver back onto roads that will help build your future and take you to the positive places you have dreamed for yourself.

Stage One: Distraction – *Distractions turn your focus away from your dreams.*

On the journey toward fulfilling their dreams, most people get distracted or at least tempted to be side-tracked. Whether the distraction is simply staying out with friends longer than you should before studying for your Spanish final or it is stressing over your relationship with your girlfriend and letting it distract you from getting your rest for the next big football game, distractions can affect anyone. Distractions happen when we turn our focus away from pursuing our dreams or goals, and we give our attention to something else. **The length of time you allow the distraction to continue will dictate the level of impact.** For example, if you decided to really work hard at school this year and make the honor roll for the first time and then after eight weeks of studying, doing your homework, and avoiding old habits you suddenly start hanging out with friends at the skate park after school instead of doing your homework, you are being distracted.

To snap out of being distracted, you have to ask yourself three questions. "*What am I distracted by? How much of a negative impact will this have on me? Am I okay with the outcomes?*" Let's go through each question using the example above. **Question 1: What are you distracted by?** *"Right now, I am spending too much time with my friends, and it is standing in the way of getting good grades."* **Question 2: How much of a negative impact will this have on me?** *"My grades will slip if I do not hand in my homework. I will also lose my weekend* privileges and possibly get benched on the football team for failing grades."

Question 3: Am I okay with the outcomes? *"No, I have worked too hard to qualify for the state championship game. I have a chance to travel with the varsity football team this year, and I do not want to mess it up."* **Always understand that you have a choice.** Nobody forces you to choose good or bad. **You make choices, and you must live with your choices.**

If you can turn away from the distractions before you create worse situations, you are demonstrating you are mature. Remember, maturity is being responsible for doing the right things even when you do not feel like it. Do this: Visualize what you want. *A good report card. Being on the varsity football team.* **Whatever it is, focus your mind on it.** Now visualize the consequences of getting distracted. *Repeating classes, you failed. Sitting down explaining to your parents. Losing car privileges.* You want to avoid negative consequences. Think about the negative results of being distracted and the problems that could result. Distractions are always around you. They must be managed. This is where discipline comes in.

D2W Character Scenario

Greg was called into his school counselor's office and learned he needed to make up six additional credits for the classes he failed. His new part-time job was taking up all his time. He had already saved up $1,000 in the first three months. He was distracted from his schoolwork because he was so focused on saving enough money to buy his car before spring break. He was getting close to saving $3,000. He was already working 20 hours per week, but he wanted to increase to 30 hours per week. His school counselor continued to share with him the impact of being distracted and not making his school work a priority.

Stage Two: Delay – *Delays reduce speed and slow progress without actually stopping.*

When you remain distracted for a period of time, you can get to a place in your life where you are delayed from achieving your dreams. This is stage two. It is now taking you longer to accomplish your dreams. Being delayed does not mean you have stopped pursuing your goals or that you have given up, but you definitely do not express the passion and commitment you once had. It is not uncommon to lose a little interest and take it a little slower. You have to be careful with stage two because being delayed can be discouraging. The risk of giving up on yourself and your dreams is a real threat. This is more than a break that everyone needs once in a while. Delays can be destructive. These situations are very easy to get started, but hard to get out of. Whatever delays you from pursuing your dreams is probably not a better choice for your life. Sometimes a delay cannot be avoided, but if your dreams are important, you have to protect your time and make the best choices.

Let's continue to work on the scenario from above.

D2W Character Scenario

Greg was now working 30 hours weekly at his part-time job. He also missed several after-school tutoring sessions at the library. His homework was behind two weeks for his Chemistry and Trigonometry classes. He also missed several basketball practices. He continued to focus his attention on saving up for his car and nothing else.

Stage Three: Detours – *Detours are a turn from a path and a change in direction.*

Detours are seen as negatives when you are on a destructive road because you have turned away and heading down a different path or direction. You might not have given up on your dreams altogether, but it is taking you longer, and you are not making significant progress. Your dreams have taken a backseat. Your time and attention are on other things. These other things do not always have to be a complete waste of time or destructive, but they steal your focus and time away from the dreams and goals you were committed to. Whatever you are doing is not moving you closer to your dreams. Many times, when young adults are detoured from what they want to pursue in their lives, they spend a lot of money and time doing things they are not passionate about. In fact, their dreams are usually covered and clouded by a lot of insignificant activity. Everything is superficial and not tied to their value system. You are moved away from your commitments.

While you are on a detour, you can be tempted to make critical decisions to fill the emptiness and create a new focus. You make decisions out of desperation as you move further away from where you want to be. Detours are not easy to endure because at some point you become aware that your dreams and goals are further from your grasp. This is not the place you want to be, but you stay here because you believe you do not have other choices and you cannot get back where you were before. You feel paralyzed and powerless to change your direction. Your fears may be the motivator of the decisions you choose now. You might start new friendships, interests, and jobs just to fill the gap created. These are not usually your best choices.

Let's continue to work on the scenario from above.

D2W Character Scenario

Now that Greg had saved up $2,500 for his car, he was more determined than ever to keep working to maintain his car and new responsibilities even at the risk of failing his Chemistry and Trigonometry classes. His school counselors warned him about his misplaced priorities. His parents and basketball coach were now also on his case. He dropped out of the basketball team. He spent every hour at his job that he could. He did not have time for his friends or his girlfriend anymore. He was considering quitting school and testing for his GED. He questioned the point of school since he desired to be a businessman anyway. School seemed like a waste of time to him.

Stage Four: Dead-Ends – *Dead-ends are the ends of a passage. It is a point beyond movement or progress.*

When you are at a dead-end, there is no more progress. You have stopped. You cannot move forward. Dead-ends are those experiences where you feel as if your life has ended. When it comes to the 4D experiences, this is the last stop on a destructive road. You have moved all the way from being distracted, delayed, detoured, and now, because you have not changed your actions, reset your focus, continued to make bad choices, or compromised your dreams, you find yourself in a place where you feel your life has hit a dead-end.

Don't get confused by the earlier lesson on the 3C's: Crashes, Collisions, and Catastrophes. This is not the same. Both lessons show what we want to avoid, but they are different. The 3C's are experiences you do not necessarily create because of unproductive behavior or bad choices. The dead-end experience is a result of wrong choices and a continual refusal to change behavior and decisions. It has a lot to do with not handling life in a responsible, mature way. Your outcomes from your decisions while on a destructive road are now becoming evident. *Being kicked out of school. Teen pregnancy. Drug addictions. Failed relationships. Family problems.* This is what happens if you stay on a destructive road. It may take weeks, months, or even years to experience the negative outcomes, but you finally wake up feeling unsettled about your life and your accomplishments. **You expected more, and you are not living the life you want to live.**

I can hear you now. *Why did I let this happen? How could I be so stupid?* Have you ever said those words to yourself? Before you beat yourself up for allowing yourself to get so off-track, realize that everyone experiences moments in their life where they question if their life is working. Remember, life is a journey of experiences. It is not uncommon for young people to have a period in their lives where they seem to go from a "good kid" making great grades and having "good friends" to the complete opposite such as failing in areas that used to be important. It happens more than we realize. It is better to keep a healthy balance in life and not make these costly mistakes, but if and when they happen, you need to know how to deal with life and move on.

When you finally recognize that you are at a dead-end, you might be depressed, confused, angry, or even indifferent. It is a place of hopelessness. A human experience not uncommon to most people, even the ones you know. Your next step is to reach out to people who can assist and encourage you to believe and start again. This might be parents, siblings, friends, co-workers, counselors, or someone you do not know personally. Anyone who builds your heart to believe again in your dreams is a valued resource. **By facing your dead-end experience, you reset your commitments in your dreams. It is time to rebuild and restart**. Personal growth starts when you come to your senses and realize you are not living the life you want and you reach out for hope to start again. That is real. Ask the older adults around you. Life is for the brave at heart. Being D2W means you embrace life. You do not sugar-coat it. You get real about what it takes and prepare yourself.

D2W Character Scenario

After five months, Greg's employer let him go. He had his new car, but now his life had hit a wall. His counselor asked him and his parents to come in for a consultation to explain how Greg did not have enough school credits to graduate with his classmates. The only way to get his high school diploma was to go to an alternative school and retake the two failed classes online while he took his regular classes. He would not be able to go to any of the senior class events. Greg was overwhelmed and depressed by the news.

In our scenario, were you able to see how the D2W character Greg progressively moved from distractions, delays, detours, and finally a dead-end? You do not just wake up and find yourself on a destructive road. You have to make one bad decision after another. The way you get off a destructive road is the same way you got on it in the first place. Make a better decision in the opposite direction. Recommit to your DREAM Clouds. **What do you want to BE? What do you want to HAVE? What do you want to EXPERIENCE**? *Do you really* *want it? Are you willing to work for your dreams?* If so, stop making decisions that create the 4D experiences. When you go in the opposite direction of your dreams, you are entering roads that take you away from where you say you want to be. Answer the next three questions: **Where are you NOW? Where are you GOING? What do I NEED to get there?** Get some direction. Create a roadmap that leads to your dreams and goals. It sounds simple. The D2W Life Management System is simple. Doing the hard work and living it out is the hard part. Life is not perfect. Life has to be managed. Learn the D2W system and work at it. **Be D2W. Be Driven 2 Win. It's your life.**

D2W Stop Sign Alert

Everyone has driven down destructive roads in their life. Sometimes we make personal decisions that lead us on roads that move us away from our dreams and goals. We create these experiences. Do not blame others; it is our fault when we make wrong decisions. Figure out how you got there; learn from the experience; and start moving in a positive direction again. Do not lose hope. Do not stay stuck. By changing your decisions, you will change your results.

D2W Assignment: It's Your Turn

List a 4D experience you have had. Identify the dream or goal. Identify what distracted you, how were you delayed, what detours did you make, and what was the impact of the dead-end experience.

What is the dream or goal?_____

What distracted you?_____

How were you delayed?_____

What detours did you make?_____

What was the impact of the dead-end experience?_____

_____

Section Two:

THE DRIVER'S HANDBOOK

Life is more manageable when we learn how we work as individuals. This information equips us with inside knowledge that we need to make better life choices. Life is not only about the journey that happens on the road, but also the inward journey to understand who we are and what we believe about ourselves. We look to the outside to provide answers, but it is said that what is happening on the outside of us first happens on the inside of us. Understanding how you operate as a person is a tremendous advantage toward personal success.

Lesson 6: Check Under the Hood

When you pop the hood up in a car, you see the engine, spark plugs, battery, etc. You see all the parts that make the car run. If the parts are in good working order, then the car should run fine. If there are faulty parts that need to be replaced or repaired, then the car's performance will suffer. The same is true with you. In life, you have to 'Check Under the Hood.' Who are you? How are you built and wired on the inside? What are you made of? Are you tuned up? That is what this lesson is about. When do people actually take the time and ask about who you are and what is important to you? Even more important, when do you ask the same questions of yourself? If you are like most people, you do not take the time to inventory and investigate what is important to you. You just jump right into life, start the engine, and start driving.

How can you start making important decisions that will shape your life before you discover who you are? How can you seriously answer the DREAM Cloud questions (What do I want to BE? What do I want to HAVE? What do I want to EXPERIENCE?) if you have not figured out what is important to you? All these insights are locked on the inside of you or "under the hood." When I say, 'Check Under the Hood' I am saying get to know who you are before you 'pave the road' to your future. **You cannot unlock your potential to its maximum level until you are fully aware of who you are and what you are made of.**

Have you figured out your VIPC profile? What does that mean? **'V' stands for Values. 'I' stands for Interests. 'P' stands for Personality traits. 'C' stands for Character traits.** Values, interests, personality traits and character traits are important factors to understand about yourself. This self-knowledge can help you make better decisions about your life and understand what opportunities are best for you. When you know more about yourself, you can build a life consistent with how you are shaped instead of creating a life not aligned to who you are.

Your VIPC profile is not set in stone. It expands as you grow as a person if you make it your mission to keep growing and being challenged. You cannot become stagnant. You have to live and experience new opportunities. Do not become trapped into small thinking and small living. Tip: You might have to leave some people behind. They might not be as adventurous and ready to travel at your speed.

Let me show you how the VIPC profile works. If you know a person who loves animals and is passionate about animal rights, they might start volunteering at an animal shelter. As they explore their career interests and research more, they might decide to pursue a career as a veterinarian or work with animals in some capacity. This career choice would support and align to their VIPC profile. **Values -** *They value animal rights.* **Interests –** *They are interested in working with animals.* **Personality traits –** *They are passionate, caring, and fun-loving.* **Character traits –** *They are determined, responsible, full of integrity, and mature.* **Do you see how the VIPC profile works?** Your VIPC profile is important because these factors impact your ability to be a successful and fulfilled person. It also will help you when choosing a career, friends, a partner, or organizations to be involved with.

Values are the things that are important to you. *What do you value?* Examples are your faith, family, friendships, good grades, being generous and kind, wealth, health, etc. Your values are 'under the hood,' and even if you are unaware of them, they are the source of your motivation. **Values are the 'WHY' you do what you do.** When you make good or bad decisions values are the reason for your choices.

You cannot say "I value education" and then refuse to study for your Algebra test or, even worse, quit school. You cannot say "I value being healthy and fit" and never exercise. Your actions are the opposite of what you acknowledge is important to you. Life works better when your values are consistent and aligned with how you behave or live your life. Your lifestyle and your choices should match your values. You do not change your values to match your lifestyle. Your lifestyle is shaped by what you value. For the most part, values stay fixed. However, when we grow as individuals, acquire new information about life, and discover new insights, our values can be enhanced, shifted, or created.

When you want to change something in your life, you will have to 'Check Under the Hood.' Your value system will have to support the changes you want to make. If you want better relationships, then you will have to value family and friends. If you want to be healthier, you will have to value your health. How you were raised and what you were exposed to also affect and influence your values. You are the owner of your values. Your upbringing and outside influences will impact you, but you ultimately have the final say on what is important to you. Nobody gets to force you and make you think and choose a certain way. If they did, then you would not be authentic and true to yourself. Remember who is in the driver's seat.

Your VIPC profile includes your interests. Interests are the activities you are involved in, like doing, and excited to learn more about. What are you interested in? Being a musician? Martial Arts? Poetry? Singing? Chess? Having a full life means you have interests that keep you engaged and interested. If you work diligently, your interests might lead you to a career or business opportunity. Interests are also areas to be recognized and rewarded for your talents. Most lasting friendships are with the people who share your interests. Relationships are an important factor if you want to "win" in life. You can see why developing interests are so important. Connect with others and build valuable relationships through your interests. You feel alone when you do not share your life with others and make these important connections. Search out and discover your interests.

Life is about discovering your talents and gifts and how to use them to enrich your life and others. Find things you like doing that are fun and provides a break from your responsibilities. Your interests might be a recreational activity or a hobby. Whatever it is, it needs to be cultivated. When you feel alone, bored, and despondent, check if your interests are dwindling. Exciting activities keep you from being bored. *If you are not building your life, then what are you doing?* Everyone needs to try new things and find what they are good at and what they are drawn to do. When you discover and try things that are exciting to you, you will get good at these areas.

When you are good at something, others will notice. I like to ask people what they are good at and what they love to do. Many people are too shy to answer, or they have not cultivated any dominant interests. *"Me? What do you mean?"* It is amazing how shy people can be when you ask them to speak about themselves and share what they are good at. Sometimes a person may be confident in sharing about themselves and express *"I am good at soccer, basketball, or writing."* You need to know what you are good at and what you like to do with your free time. Do not make the mistake of not being involved in anything. Your life is much more exciting when you stay engaged and have things to do that you enjoy. You only get one life. Fill it up with excitement.

The next area of the VIPC profile starts with the letter 'P,' which stands for personality traits. If you asked your closest friends to name three words that describe your personality traits what would they say? People close to you know you. Are you energetic, shy, inquisitive, or funny? Would your friends in your sports league say that you are aggressive or playful? Personality traits are the qualities that describe who you are and what you are like. Personality traits do not usually change as you get older. They can be developed further, though. Your personality traits might guide you to make better career choices. Have you ever taken a personality trait test and found out some things about yourself? This can be a fun discovery, especially when you are also evaluating your friends. You might be adventurous and courageous, and your best friend might be practical and serious. We are different. People close enough to your life are observing you. We are not always aware of how we are being perceived by others.

If you are shy and quiet, it does not mean you cannot respond as a confident person in certain situations, but normally you will consistently demonstrate your dominant qualities. If you are friendly and caring, how does that show up in your life with others? Do you find yourself helping your family and friends? Do you look out for others? This will definitely help with making friends. Be careful though. Even positive personality traits like being friendly and nice can backfire on you. People might think you are a pushover and "too friendly and nice" and will try to take advantage of you.

All of us have personality traits that make us shine and other qualities really bring the worst outcomes in our lives. You might be funny, but conceited. Negative personality traits need to be worked on. If you were described as conceited, anxious, self-absorbed, these qualities would not help you "win" in life. You might create a lot of problems for yourself and with others. People might not want to deal with you for long. We should always work on becoming our best person. That means we need to be honest, and find ways to improve how we live our lives.

The last area of the VIPC profile starts with the letter 'C,' which stands for character traits. Character traits are a little different than personality traits. The difference is that character traits describe your behavior or how you act in a situation, not simply your inner

qualities. Sometimes you might confuse character traits with personality traits, but a way to distinguish between the two is that anyone can develop positive character traits and behaviors. Everyone can demonstrate they are determined, respectful, eager, assertive, and motivated. That is the major difference. Not everyone can be humorous or inquisitive, but everyone can be diligent or responsible. See the difference? Character traits are a huge factor in personal success.

An inquisitive person is a curious person. They are always searching and asking questions. Now someone that is honest tells the truth. They do not make it a practice to lie. This is a character trait. It describes a behavior. Being honest is important to relationships, keeping a job, and being a well-adjusted person. Everyone should strive to be honest because your life will be more successful. It does not matter what personality traits you possess, you can always choose to be an honest person.

Let's look at another comparison. Are you shy? Are you assertive? Not everyone is shy, but everyone can demonstrate being assertive. Can you be shy and assertive at the same time? *"I am shy. I do not speak up without anxiety as others. I do not really care for experiences where I am in the spotlight."* This does not mean you cannot be assertive when necessary. If you need an internship and make an appointment to see your career counselor, then you are being assertive. For that specific situation, you are demonstrating that you are being assertive to be successful even though you are a shy person.

Developing positive character traits is the most productive way to advance in life. You may not have all the advantages as others. You might not be voted 'Most Likely to Succeed' at your school. However, people who "build the dream on the inside," meaning they demonstrate successful character traits, attract and "unlock" opportunities in their life by having a VIPC profile made up of winning character traits.

Your VIPC profile is an area where you can develop and prepare yourself to "win" in life. When you 'Check Under the Hood,' you are working on your values, interests, personality traits, and character traits. When you grow as a person, your VIPC profile grows. It is important to take the time to discover and examine these important areas. They will help you make better decisions and guide you to pursue opportunities that support the person you are on the inside.

D2W Character Scenario

Everyone always said Antonio was the nicest guy. He was caring, a little shy, and the most dependable friend. He valued his family and friends and was loyal. When Eliza was having a tough time in her Algebra class, Antonio tutored her for weeks until her grades were raised. Antonio was the oldest sibling, and he had several brothers and sisters. He was always taking care of them and concerned with others. When he said that he considered a career as a pediatrician, everyone thought his caring personality would be perfect. His career counselor helped him research the best universities and scholarships.

D2W Stop Sign Alert

It is important to continually develop and check your values, interests, personality traits, and character traits. Your progress in life is largely based on what is happening 'under the hood' or inside you. Make sure you not only pay attention to what is happening around you, but also figure out what is happening on the inside.

Identify three of your top values, interests, personality traits, and character traits.

Ask a friend to name three in each category. Determine if there are any matches.

	Values	Interests	Personality traits	Character traits
1.	————	————	————	————
2.	————	————	————	————
3.	————	————	————	————

Friend's answers

1.	————	————	————	————
2.	————	————	————	————
3.	————	————	————	————

Lesson 7: Steer Toward Your Goals

Are you ready to drive? What is your dream car? Can you see yourself in it? Drivers have privileges that passengers do not have. Drivers set goals for where they want to go and what they want to accomplish in life. Be a 'driver' in your life; refuse to be a passenger. **Steer toward the goals that are important to you.** Don't let life happen to you. You influence Life. Don't let Life take you places where you do not have a say in the matter. Remember what the word 'ownership' means? Ownership was the first rule listed in the 'Ten Golden Rules of the Road.' Do not give your 'ownership' away by being casually okay with everything that comes your way. Drivers take responsibility for their lives and understand that their decisions set the course for their lives. Be a driver. Take the steering wheel of life and determine your course by setting your goals.

I met a young man who was around 23 years old. He was working as a security guard and had been there for some months. He was living in his parent's home off and on and seemingly still dependent. I asked him what his dream was. He shared that he was interested in pursuing a career in the home decorating industry. His eyes sparked when he spoke about it. He had this dream ever since graduating high school, but he gave it up because his dad convinced him there was no future stability in that industry and encouraged him to pursue computer engineering. He did exactly what his dad wanted and started college, but months into the program he was not inspired enough to keep up. He dropped out of school and worked at low-paying jobs for years. He wasted about 4 to 5 years not connected to his passion or interests.

For years, he was not courageous enough to pursue his passion. It was apparent he did not want to be where he was. I shared with him what being D2W was all about and how your dreams can come true when you are brave enough to set your goals and be true to yourself. A few weeks later, I spoke to him again, and he shared that he had a honest conversation with his dad and got the courage to pursue a college degree in the home decorating industry. He was full of excitement because he was weeks away from flying back to his country Colombia to pursue his passion. You should have seen him the last week at his security guard job. He was so happy and inspired. This is what connecting to your dream will do for you. I told him I was proud of him for finally having the courage to pursue his dream again.

You must protect your passion. Do not let the 'play-if-safe' people in the world steal your dream. Explore and investigate life, and when you have discovered your passion and dream, get on a path and drive forward. You should always show up strong in your own life. When people continually act like passengers in life, they normally have serious regrets on how their life has turned out. Understand it's up to you and that is a good thing. If it was up to someone else, you would not have control, and you could blame them for not accomplishing your goals. There can be only one person in the driver's seat, and that is you.

You can tell when someone has given up on a dream they had for their lives. You can spot them. They speak about their past with regret. They talk about what did not happen instead of what they actually accomplished. You can sense and feel the regret in their words for not experiencing what could have been. They have become comfortable with what they have today. It is not as if they did not have any goals or did not accomplish anything, but there is always that huge goal or that big challenge that escapes you. **When you stop pushing**

forward, you stop moving. Life tries to push you into a corner and make you stop short of your greatness. The question is, *"Will you win or will you lose?" Will you break your stride or will you push to make it to the next level? Will you die with your dream and forget you ever had that spark in your eye?* **Now, before you think I do not live in the real world, let me say this. If you are in the 'driver's seat,' it is your privilege to determine where you are going. You may decide that you have arrived at the destination you set for yourself and achieved your goals.** If you have, then it is your right to become comfortable and satisfied with your accomplishments. However, if there is even the slightest bit of discomfort or dissatisfaction with where you are, then listen to the voice inside you because you are not finished. Get moving. The journey continues. Stop resting. Push forward and attain. WIN BIG. WIN NOW.

Life is filled with opportunities and potential when you set your goals. Goals give you something to focus on. It takes time and a lot of hard work. Accomplishing your goals is challenging, but it is worth the effort. You become stronger and more confident as you pursue your goals. It is not always pleasant, but don't shrink because of the challenges you face. **For every challenge, you must be the challenger. Challenge the status quo in your life. Grab Faith not Fear. Steer toward your goals. Live a life of fulfillment. Keep pushing until what you are living is your DREAM.**

D2W Character Scenario

Greg wanted so badly to go to Europe with Michael and his friends for spring vacation, but it cost $1,200 for the trip. He had already saved $2,500 toward his car purchase. His savings were low, but he really wanted to go. He could not save that much money from his part-time job that quickly. Now, this was another goal. His dad said he would contribute half the money, but that meant Greg had to find a way to save $600 in the next three months. All his talk about being a businessman didn't mean anything if he could not find a solution. He talked to his business teacher and shared his dilemma. For his classroom project, Greg was working on a business idea to sell personalized cell phone products. Once, he made a prototype of the personalized cell phone case everyone in school wanted one. He was placing dozens of orders. Before, long Greg had the $800 and much more. He definitely proved to himself and his friends he was serious about his goals.

D2W Stop Sign Alert

It takes courage and a determined mind to pursue your dreams and goals. It is easy to quit and give up. Nothing worth having just falls into your lap. The journey toward the goal is the real value because you become stronger in the process. You are worth the effort. Give your best and shake off the discouragement. Determine the goal and set the course. Keep moving and striving. One step forward is one step closer.

D2W Assignment: It's Your Turn

Write down three of your current goals. On a scale of 1 to 5, 5 being the highest, rate how motivated and focused you are toward pursuing your goals. Answer the question of why your goals are important to you. Have a friend and one adult to complete this exercise. Compare responses.

My goals	Rate	Why is this goal important to you?
1. _____	_____	_____
2. _____	_____	_____
3. _____	_____	_____

Friend's goals	Rate	Why is this goal important to them?
1. _____	_____	_____
2. _____	_____	_____
3. _____	_____	_____

Adult's goals	Rate	Why is this goal important to them?
1. _____	_____	_____
2. _____	_____	_____
3. _____	_____	_____

Lesson 8: Put Your Life in Gear

Once you make up your mind and set goals, you will be faced with decisions. Making decisions is similar to putting your life in gear. Sometimes you have several options to consider. You set a goal to pursue a college degree. Will you pursue a medicine, engineering, or finance degree? What do you do when there are several decisions worth considering? There is no wrong or right answer. **All are options; however, your dreams, your VIPC profile, and your goals will determine which gear or which decision to choose.** When you drive a car, there are four primary gears. Will you put the car in **Park**, **Reverse**, **Neutral**, or **Drive**? These four gears represent decisions that you will make as you drive your dreams forward. Will you 'park' your goal to lose excess weight and exercise at the gym three times per week and slack off? Will you put your life in 'reverse' and make the decision to hang out with kids on your block smoking marijuana on the weekend instead of catching the bus to go to your part-time job? Will you put the gear in 'drive' and go straight to college after high school to pursue your education? **Life demands you make decisions. You cannot "win" in life if you are unwilling to make solid decisions and take action to create the life you want. Success starts with a decision.**

When you have researched and decided you want something, put the gear in 'drive.' Get your head out of the clouds. Stop daydreaming. Do not hesitate. How long are you going to talk about what you want and what you are going to do? You keep telling your family you are going to get a part-time job. Then do it. You keep wishing you were the one that was going to state championships. Do what it takes to get there. When I say, 'Put Your Life in Gear,' that means move out of 'park' into 'drive' by making the decisions and performing the actions that will get you where you want to be. It is not enough to talk about being the first person in your family to go to college or start a business. First, set the goal. Next, make smart decisions that support those goals. It takes effort to experience success in any capacity. Real committed, focused effort is how to succeed in life. Your life is happening right now. Make it count!!!

Are you giving up on your goals if you put the gear in 'neutral?' 'Neutral' is not necessarily a negative gear. There are times when the 'neutral' gear represents the best decision at that specific time. When driving, the 'neutral' gear is used when you want to coast down the hill and save gas. In life, you might use the 'neutral' gear when you are unsure what your next move should be. For example, if you get accepted at two different colleges, and you have to decide which college you want to go to, you cannot be hasty and make a decision until you get more information. You might need to research and compare college programs, the cost, campus life, or the student-to-teacher ratios to make an informed decision. Move out of 'neutral' once you are confident with your decision.

Some people refuse to take action, and they wait until they are forced to make decisions. Do you need pain to help motivate you? What is it going to take for you to make the right decision? A power talk? A friend to encourage you? Problems? Bad situations? Decide right now that you will be a disciplined person and will not wait until you are backed into a corner to make the necessary decisions. For example, the D2W character Antonio struggles with his weight and has hired a fitness trainer. Does he make the daily decision to stay focused on his health and fitness goals or does he wait until his doctor warns him about diabetes? Being D2W means we do not allow bad circumstances to move us to make the right decisions. **We make decisions that lead us forward.** Pretend the D2W Character Janice has to make a decision to stay at her old ballet school or enroll in a new school with instructors who can help advance her skills. If Janice wants to improve her skills, she should put the gear in 'drive' and find the right ballet instructors even if the decision is difficult.

Being in the driver's seat means you will be required to set goals and make decisions. Life rewards decisive people. <u>Indecision should be uncomfortable to you</u>. You cannot move forward in 'park' or 'neutral.' Own your decisions. Even if you make bad decisions, you have the opportunity to grow and learn from them. Every time you are in a car, look at the gearshift and think about your decisions. Are you being courageous and mature, and making decisions that will help you move forward? Being D2W means you make decisions even when they are difficult. You should be proud of yourself for every decision that moves you forward. Refuse to be stuck, depressed, or detoured from your dreams and goals. **Your dreams and goals will not become a reality until you are brave enough to make decisions.**

D2W Character Scenario

Eliza decided she would submit her internship application for the Mayor's Youth Leadership Advisory Council position. She was anxious to get the call for an interview after waiting three weeks. She had decided she would pursue this opportunity when her career counselor shared about careers in the political industry. She practiced the interview questions diligently that her career counselor gave her. She put her favorite dress in the cleaners. When she got the call for the interview, Eliza made sure her mom knew the date and time, so she had a ride to the Mayor's office.

D2W Stop Sign Alert

Decisions are made every day. Put your life in gear by making up your mind. You are responsible for your path. Be careful not to let people rush you into making decisions. Do your homework and research first. Do not be indecisive and take forever on making a decision. Get the knowledge and support you need. When you make a wrong decision, do not be discouraged; simply get better information to make decisions that help you arrive at your destination.

D2W Assignment: It's Your Turn

Rewrite your three goals below. (Refer back to Lesson 7.) Identify the "gear" that you are in.

GOAL #1 _____ GEAR: _____

GOAL #2 _____ GEAR: _____

GOAL #3 _____ GEAR: _____

Lesson 9: Control Yourself: How are you performing?

How do you determine if your life is working? What criteria do you use? How do you determine whether you are on track and accomplishing your goals? There is a way to find the answers to these questions, and the secret is using the gauges on the car's control panel. When you sit in a car, look at the control panel. These controls are on the dashboard and represent five important areas to monitor and evaluate car performance. **The five control panel gauges are: 1) fuel gauge, 2) speedometer, 3) tachometer, 4) temperature gauge, and 5) odometer.** Each control gauge has its own purpose and provides information necessary to solve car problems and evaluate performance. In life, these same controls represent important **The fuel gauge represents <u>resources</u> you will need while pursuing your dreams and goals.** This is the first control area. Resources are money, mentors, counselors, scholarships, training programs, etc. Have your parents ever run out of gas with you in the car? When you are close to running out of gas, there is usually a flashing light and an annoying sound to warn you. Well, Life also gives you signs and reminders when you are running low on your resources. **What resources do you need to accomplish your goals?** Remember the question 'What do you need to get there?' The fuel gauge represents all the resources or things you need to be successful on your journey. In most cases, the problems or challenges you face are related to acquiring resources. What problems do you face related to your dreams and goals? If you are planning to go to college, you will need money, scholarships, and financial aid. If you are learning how to play the guitar, you will need a guitar and guitar lessons, which also will require money. Whatever the dream or goal, resources will be required, which means your problem or challenge is to obtain them if you want to be successful. You will always need resources. **Do not let the lack of resources stop or halt your dreams and goals.** It is just another area to manage and evaluate. Resources serve the purpose of your dreams and goals. They will find you if you stay focused on where you are going and do not give up.

The speedometer represents the <u>pace</u> **or time management skills you demonstrate while pursuing your dreams and goals.** This is the second control area. Look at the speedometer in a car. It tells you how fast or slow the car is going, and it represents pacing yourself as you stay committed. What is the fastest speed you have ever gone in a car? 80 miles per hour? 100 miles per hour? Cars usually flip over if you try to turn a corner more than 70 miles per hour. **Going too fast means you are not managing your schedule to be successful with your tasks. Going too slow means you are not working diligently enough to make significant progress.**

<u>Time management is one of the biggest challenges to living out your dreams because you need wisdom to organize the work and the patience to stay encouraged when success does not come as quickly as you think it should</u>. You need time management skills to pace yourself and prioritize the tasks that you are capable of handling. It is difficult to stay motivated or enthusiastic when it seems like you are not getting closer to accomplishing your goals. It takes strong character traits like discipline and resilience to stay the course and manage your step-by-step actions. Build your momentum and move your life ahead by keeping the right pace.

The tachometer represents the <u>effort</u> **required as you pursue your dreams and goals.** This is the third control area. It measures the effort the engine has to work to move the car forward. Are you doing what it takes to get to your next step? Give your best effort. When you study for a test, evaluate your effort. Grades are usually an indication of your level of effort. If you make a good grade, you can be proud of yourself. Even when you studied diligently and did not make a good grade, you still can be proud you did your best. Always assess yourself and be honest.

I met a young high school student walking at school holding a basketball, and I asked him if he was a good player. He shared that he recently tried out for the varsity team and almost made it. I could tell that was an important goal for him. He was proud of his efforts. He seemed young for the varsity team. I could tell that basketball was his life, and he was committed to being an exceptional player. What are you working toward right now? Are you doing what it takes to succeed? Winning is more than coming in first. Your biggest win will be when you make the effort to be your personal best. Do not slack off. Check the controls.

The temperature gauge represents your <u>attitude</u> **while pursuing your dreams and goals**. This is the fourth control area. Your attitude is your perspective and the way you think and feel about something. The best attitude is essential to creating the right environment to win in life. This is one of the strongest determinants of personal success. Are you excited, confident, and encouraged? Are you pessimistic, indifferent, and disappointed? These attitudes can affect your ability to stay strong and focused on your goals. **How you think and feel about yourself and your life will control how far you will go in life.** I am sure you are excited when you get a wage increase at your part-time job. You are encouraged when your coach recommends you for the varsity team. Use these same attitudes for the difficult times. **When you fail, check your attitude. Choose the attitude that will help you win.** When you are passed up for the scholarship, learned you did not get the lead part in the play, or scored lower than you wanted on the SAT Exam, continue to be enthusiastic and confident. <u>A sign of maturity is regulating your attitude</u>. Stay encouraged. Think good thoughts. Do not speak negative words when you are angry, frustrated, and sad. It is not easy to stay positive, but keep pushing through the pain. Positive thoughts lead to positive attitudes. Negative thoughts lead to negative attitudes. Focus your thoughts on your future success. Check the controls. Check your attitude.

The odometer represents your <u>progress</u> **as you pursue your dreams and goals**. This is the fifth control area. Do you know what the odometer looks like? It is the control that shows how many miles you have driven in your car. Most car engines can go up to approximately 300,000 miles if you take care of the car. **Are you progressing toward your dreams and goals? Do you feel proud of your accomplishments? Is your hard work making**

a difference? It is great when you review your life, and you can see progress. Did all those extra football practices with the coach make a difference in the game? Did going to tutoring for the past six weeks help raise your English grade? Everyone wants to progress when they work hard to achieve something. If you are putting in the effort, but still not progressing, you have to ask yourself why. An effective way to figure out what is happening is to check the other controls. Your progress might be halted due to the other control areas related to resources, time management, effort, and even attitude. Progress feels good when you have worked hard. Progress means you are satisfied with yourself and actually achieving and experiencing what you planned.

Success requires that you manage and evaluate your resources, time, effort, attitude, and progress. All these control areas are predictors of success or failure at any dream and goal. Most of the problems you will face will fall into these five control areas. Once you understand each control area individually, you then will be ready to evaluate how they work together. They will tell the story of your performance. If your resources are inadequate, you cannot progress as you would like to. If you are pacing yourself and you are progressing, your effort and attitude will be strong. If you are managing your time well, then your resources will be used adequately. All these control areas work together, and all of them are strong indicators for successful performance.

D2W Character Scenario

Michael had three weeks to prepare for the varsity football tryouts. Everyone thought he had a chance, but he wondered if he was really good enough to make the team. He called up his old football coach and let him know he needed some extra workouts for precision and conditioning. He started practicing four hours on the weekends in addition to his regular school football practices. His coach was really proud of him and let him know he improved tremendously. Michael was excited about his progress. He had put a lot of effort into his sport. His throws were sharper, and he was faster than before. He was ready.

D2W Stop Sign Alert

Success does not simply happen on its own. Resources, time management, effort, attitude, and progress are essential factors of success for any endeavor. You should develop a habit of checking your performance in the five control areas. This is a proactive way to keep performing well and managing potential problems.

D2W Assignment: It's Your Turn

Rewrite one of your current goals. (Refer back to Lesson 7) Identify a problem you might be experiencing. Answer the control panel questions to solve problems and evaluate your performance.

GOAL: _____ PROBLEM: _____

RESOURCES: What resources do you need? _____

PACE: How is your pace and time management? _____

EFFORT: What level of effort are you giving? _____

ATTITUDE: How is your attitude? _____

PROGRESS: How is your progress? _____

Section 3:

TOOLS OF LIFE

It would be great if life just worked effortlessly without any need of repairs or maintenance; however, as with cars, life does not work like that. It demands continual maintenance and sometimes repairs. Without effort and dedication, everything breaks down. Using effective tools is essential to keep life working well. Whether you are changing the oil, replacing an old battery, changing tires, or fixing engine problems, you must use the right tools. A tool is anything you use to help you do a certain work or produce a result.

In life, we need tools to assist with gaining information, increasing performance, and solving problems. To maintain and enhance life performance, there are four D2W Life Management tools: **Character-Building, Goal-Setting, Decision-Making, and Problem-Solving/Evaluation**. When these tools are used together, they activate the D2W Life Management System to help manage your life and increase personal performance.

Lesson 10: Tool 1 - Character-Building

If you are going to build your future, you will have to know how important your character is. **What is your character? <u>Character is defined as the behavior, qualities, or traits that form a person's individual nature.</u>** They say everything rises and falls on your character. Your character is the foundation of everything. If it is not strong and firm, your life will ultimately collapse because of the lack of development. **Of all the factors in the VIPC profile that determine personal success, you have ultimate control over your character.** You determine how you behave. In the D2W Life Management System, character traits are described as character keys, which is one of the qualities introduced in the 'Check Under the Hood' lesson. There are two purposes for keys. They unlock doors, and they ignite or start up engines. **Character keys "unlock your dreams and ignite your passion." You open the doors of opportunity when you possess positive character traits.**

D	R	E	A	M
Diligent	Responsible	Ethical	Assertive	Mature
Determined	Resilient	Earnest	Approachable	Motivated
Decisive	Resourceful	Enthusiastic	Appreciative	Modest
Disciplined	Respectful	Encouraged	Attentive	Merciful

<u>**Character-building is the first tool in the D2W Life Management System.**</u> **Unlock the D-R-E-A-M and IGNITE the Passion. Are you building the D-R-E-A-M inside you?** If you are building the D-R-E-A-M inside, every day you wake up focused on demonstrating character traits or character keys that will help you succeed at your goals. In every situation you face, you must use the appropriate D-R-E-A-M character key combination to get to your next step. If you played football or baseball, would you need to be diligent? Would you hustle without the coach yelling for you to do so? Are you committed to working diligently on the school project

or finishing a task your employer gave you? If you answered 'Yes' to these questions, then you clearly are 'diligent' with these tasks. This means it is important for you to try your best. Pretend you have an Algebra test and you need some extra tutoring during lunch break. Use the character keys to unlock the door. Show up for the tutoring appointment on time. Use the character keys **'Diligence' 'Responsible,' Earnest,' Assertive,' and 'Motivated'** and work hard to learn the material so you can do well. Unlock your opportunities. Life rewards those that work the system.

So, what is the first step? Learn the 20 character keys in the D2W Leadership System. There are four sets of D-R-E-A-M character keys containing four words starting with each letter in the word 'DREAM.' **Are you diligent, determined, decisive, and disciplined?** Your dream will require you to demonstrate these character traits. **Are you responsible, resilient, resourceful, and respectful?** Life will give you challenges until these character traits are built in you. **Are you ethical, earnest, enthusiastic, and encouraged?** You cannot attract opportunities without these. **Are you assertive, approachable, appreciative, and attentive?** If you want to build good, stable, lasting relationships, you must demonstrate these behaviors. Last one: **Are you motivated, mature, modest, and merciful?** All of these words are important for personal success. Look at the complete list. Learn the definition of each of these words.

The second step is to assess whether you consistently demonstrate the character keys. How many of the character keys do you consistently demonstrate? Do you demonstrate the character keys only for the activities you are passionate about or do these words describe how you behave most of the time? Make these character keys a part of your everyday existence. Look at a situation or task and determine which character keys will be beneficial. Ask yourself what you can do today to demonstrate those specific character keys? Go down the list daily and commit to at least five character keys you will purposely demonstrate. Write them down. Remind yourself throughout the day of your intention. Speak to yourself: **"Today, I will be diligent at** *(fill in the blank)*. **Today, I commit to being** *(fill in the blank)*.**"** At the end of the day, review which character keys you have demonstrated. Do it again and again until it becomes automatic for you.

The best thing you can do to make your dreams a reality is build your character. It is the mark of a mature and accomplished person. **You cannot control everything in life, but you can choose how you will behave.** If you do not demonstrate positive character keys, then you will demonstrate negative ones. You are either diligent or unfaithful. You are either responsible or irresponsible. Remember this: **The journey to get what we want is filled up with the treasures of becoming who we are meant to be.** You are your character. Every time you demonstrate a character key, you move one step closer to becoming ready and qualified to possess what you seek after. You will pass every 'Test of Maturity' because you have created internal success by building your character. It is the difference between success and ultimate failure. You cannot be D2W without building your character. Be Driven 2 Win. Be D2W. You do not have to be perfect. Be your best. Your character will open the doors to your dreams. **Unlock the D-R-E-A-M and IGNITE the Passion.**

D2W Character Scenario

Michael was diligent to practice extra hours to qualify for the varsity football team. Janice was resilient to prepare for her ballet recital regardless of past disappointments. Antonio was earnest about getting the grades and scholarships he needed to go to the best medical university. Eliza was assertive when she asked her career counselor to prepare a letter of recommendation for the Mayor's internship application. Melanie was disciplined to attend her SAT study sessions and retake her SAT Test to gain higher scores. Greg was mature to find a new part-time job to earn the money he needed for his financial obligations.

D2W Stop Sign Alert

Your continued commitment to building positive character traits will benefit your life and bring good results. Try to demonstrate all 20 D-R-E-A-M character keys. Be honest about where you are in your life and identify the character strengths that will help you move closer to your dreams. Make it your mission.

D2W Assignment: It's Your Turn

Write down up to three of your DREAM Clouds. (Refer to Lesson 1.) Identify the D-R-E-A-M character keys for each DREAM Cloud you will need to demonstrate to prepare for success.

DREAM CLOUD 1: _____ D-R-E-A-M CHARACTER KEYS: _____

DREAM CLOUD 2: _____ D-R-E-A-M CHARACTER KEYS: _____

DREAM CLOUD 3: _____ D-R-E-A-M CHARACTER KEYS: _____

Lesson 11: Tool 2 - Goal-Setting

Tool 2 is about goal-setting. <u>Goal-setting is defined as the process of setting goals to achieve specific outcomes.</u> What is one of your goals for this year? Are you the kind of person who sets goals and writes them down every year? It is important for you to specify what you want to accomplish in your life. It is not enough to want to be successful. You have to plan for it. It starts by setting goals. **Winners have to set goals.** Ask any person who has succeeded at anything noteworthy if they had to set goals, list out their actions, and stay focused. **Winners focus their attention and efforts on the prize.** Accomplishing a desire is the reason a person sets goals. For example, a person who is on the swim team probably has a goal to beat a certain qualifying time or perfect a new technique that their swim coach taught them. A person on the varsity basketball team will practice and set a goal to score 12 points or more in the next game. A person interested in learning how to play chess will set a goal to learn how each piece moves.

I want to encourage you to get serious about setting goals right now. It doesn't matter how old you are. You can set goals for yourself at any age. Sometimes you do not know where to start with goal-setting. Your dreams should guide you on what goals to set for yourself. Your dreams are like clouds. They are in the sky. They cannot manifest and become a reality until you "steer toward your goals" by clearly identifying what you want to accomplish. **DREAMS come first, and then GOALS.** When you simply set random goals, you may succeed, but when you have a DREAM that is supported by your value system (Check Under the Hood), and then directed by your goals, you will be more committed to being successful.

Goals are personal. Your goals might be related to sports. They might be about your personal development, such as keeping your school folder or room clean. Maybe you set a goal to save up $200 for a field trip, or you set a goal to save up for a car. You have to go after what you want in life. That means setting goals and working hard. Things do not just fall into your lap most of the time. You cannot always depend on your parents or guardians to give you everything, and you should not want them to. As you get older and mature, you should want to do some things for yourself. It gives you a sense of pride. You can say "I did that. I made that happen."

Why is setting goals important? It is important because it focuses your energy and efforts on what you want. It forces you to decide what is important and shapes the life you want to create. You cannot do everything, or you will be ineffective. If you ask the football captain, the ASB president, or a person seeking college scholarships about accomplishing their goals, they will probably express that it requires diligence, not letting people or things distract you, and not giving up. **People who succeed must set goals, stay focused, and remain determined.**

Have your parents ever said to you, *"Grow up. You are too old for this?"* Well, your goals have to grow up, too. Not only do you need age-appropriate goals based on your maturity level, but you need what are called **stretch goals**. These are goals just beyond your reach that you really have to work hard to accomplish. Your goals will be small at first, but they become more complex as your vision grows. Do you remember when you were in kindergarten and your major goal was to get gold stars to fill up the chart your teacher gave you? At this age your goal was to read your first book by yourself. You should not be proud anymore because you can tie your shoes. I mean, yeah, at one point everyone clapped for you when you didn't fall when riding a bike and everyone thought you were great when you got an 'A' on your spelling test with four-letter words, but today your goals have to be a little more comprehensive than that. Maybe your current goal is to raise your Algebra grade from a 'C' to a 'B' or make the varsity football team. **Goals should be appropriate for your age, skill, and maturity level.** There is not much satisfaction with easy goals. Difficulty makes you stronger.

Goals also have to follow the **S-M-A-R-T rule**. Goals should be **specific**, **measurable**, **attainable**, **realistic**, and **time-specific**. You can't just say *"I want to be successful."* *"I want to lose weight." "I want to have a good life."* That does not give enough information. When you ask people about their goals, even adults sometimes express them just like that. These examples do not follow the S-M-A-R-T rule. You cannot determine when you have achieved your goals. They do not provide enough information to describe exactly what will happen, when it will happen, and the characteristics of the outcome. It is just like a fleeting cloud in the sky. You cannot grab hold of it.

Let's take these same three goal statements and learn how to set S-M-A-R-T goals. *"I want to be successful."* Success is not defined in this statement. It is not measurable. A better statement would be: *"I want to have a life where I am connected to family and friends and travel with them at least two times a year."* This statement specifically identifies that spending time with valuable people is how success is measured. Instead of *"I want to lose weight,"* it should be *"I want to lose an extra 20lbs in the next six months."* This statement passes the S-M-A-R-T rule. I now know how much weight you want to lose and how soon you want to lose it. *"I want to have a good life."* This statement could be about anything. What is a good life? It is different for each person. Is a good life related to having a healthy body, a successful career, or a fun lifestyle? If you do not define it, it will not be clear. *"I want a career that makes a full-time salary of at least $80,000 annually."* Now, this statement clearly defines what a good life is. See how much clearer the S-M-A-R-T goal statements are?

In the D2W Life Management System, there are six goal areas. Each of the D2W Characters represents one of the goals and the D2W Character Scenarios provide examples on how they manage those specific areas. Take a look at the D2W Steering Wheel Action Plan in the Appendix section. You will see the six goals individually, but they work collectively. This means they relate to and impact each other so that when you work on one goal area, it reinforces the other areas. By setting goals in these six areas, you will create a winning path toward your dreams.

 Goal 1: Personal Development – It is the process of enhancing your knowledge, skills, and experiences through access and exposure to developmental opportunities.

 Goal 2: Education (Higher Learning) – It is the process of acquiring knowledge and developing reasoning abilities of the mind through schooling, training, and study.

 Goal 3: Healthy Relationships - It is the connection and association with individuals and organizations that promote quality interaction and provide life-affirming, supportive assistance toward personal and professional growth and achievement.

 Goal 4: Health/Nutrition/Fitness - It is a lifestyle that demonstrates one's commitment to responsible health practices, good nutrition, and exercise.

 Goal 5: Financial Education/Responsibility – It is the commitment to building financial knowledge and demonstrating how to utilize money responsibly to finance personal vision and build a secure economic future.

 Goal 6: Community Involvement - It is the commitment to being knowledgeable about community needs, resources and projects as well as being involved to increase skills, provide assistance, and build relationships.

Goal 1: Personal Development

Some of you come from homes with parents who make it their priority to expose you to art, culture, traveling, or anything to enrich your life so you can yearn for bigger and better things. You are blessed. **Personal development is the process of enhancing your knowledge, skills, and experiences through access and exposure to developmental opportunities.** It is this exposure that builds a mindset that life is not boring, but should be explored. This is how you develop yourself. Are you taking advantage of all your opportunities? If you need more exposure to opportunities, you can make it happen for yourself. Who is in the Driver's Seat? You are. It is your life. Look for your opportunities. Seek them out. Do not take 'NO' for an answer. Do not let the lack of money keep you from searching. If you see a youth program that helps youth travel, and you want to travel, get involved. If you see an opportunity to go to a college campus and participate in a cool activity, then go for it. Develop an eye for the things and activities that can build you as a person. If you are not exposed or do not have access to these type of opportunities, then you will not be fully cultivated and prepared like others. If you want it badly enough, there is a road to get you there. Yes, it's difficult to create something from nothing, but when your will is stronger than your obstacles, I believe you attract opportunities in your life. That includes money.

Every day be ready for the challenge. Wake up and seize your opportunities. The person you will be competing for jobs and careers in the next five years is seeking out their opportunities right now. What are you doing? The person you might be interested in dating in the next three years is traveling to different countries, meeting new friends, and becoming a confident, self-reliant, articulate person. They will not want to share their life with a disengaged, uncultivated, insecure person who has not bothered to challenge the unknown. Become a strong, genuine, and creative person. People like attractive people. I am not speaking about how you look. Being attractive is more than how pretty or handsome you are. You are attractive when you live your life to the fullest. Be your best person. Build your life. Seize your opportunities. Move to your next level.

D2W Character Scenario

Janice read about the traveling ballet company coming to town auditioning young dancers interested in joining their organization. She loved ballet and dedicated herself to developing her talent. She set a goal to be ready for the audition in one month. She needed to hire a choreographer, find a male dance partner, and select the music and costumes. This was her chance to find out if she was talented enough to impress industry-level ballet instructors.

Goal 2: Education (Higher Learning)

I believe you understand why education is so important to your future. This is one of the major ways you qualify for your jobs, careers, and other opportunities. It is not the only way, but our society has made academic achievements a top measure of how to be promoted. **Education or higher learning is the process of acquiring knowledge and developing reasoning abilities of the mind through schooling, training, and study.** You need a sharp mind to work in information technology careers. Engineers need to have strong math and reasoning abilities. The deductive thinking you perform in your Chemistry class will come in handy one day as an adult working as a financial analyst at your company. Your formal education is the road to gain traction in your career life.

I know some of you completely pride yourselves on being the smartest person in your Advanced Placement classes. Your grade point average is probably your life. You might be the kind of person that might die if you got a 'C' on a test. Success in education is a strong indicator of future success. Your grade point average is important when it comes to getting into competitive colleges and universities. Your scores on the SAT and ACT college tests are essential. All of that is important as you progress to your next academic levels. **However, when it comes to being a successful adult, it is about the whole package.** You have to do more than pass the Algebra test or write a great essay paper for your English class. You have to win as a whole, complete person. This goal deals with your commitment to formal education, but it also challenges you to be a life learner.

Are you a life learner or are you only doing the bare minimum, hoping people get off your back and leave you alone? Are you committed to your education? A life learner wants to learn and grow continuously in new ways even when it is challenging, intimidating, or uncomfortable. Being a life learner means you are committed to being the best, sharpest person you can be. Is that you? This goes beyond someone making you sit down and pay attention in a classroom. There is a great quote that states, *"Don't let your education get in the way of your learning."* My question to you: When all the parents, teachers, and high school counselors are gone, and it is just you alone sitting with your dreams and goals, will you have the discipline to focus in on your education and attain your college degrees because you decided it is important for your future? Many people start college, but not all of them finish.

Soon, nobody will be forcing you to go to school. You will make the decisions and navigate the turns in your life. I wonder what roads, what decisions, you will make when it comes to your education and higher learning. I wonder do you have what it takes to stay focused and build a secure future. Who's in the driver's seat? YOU ARE!!!

D2W Character Scenario

Michael was always consumed with being the best on the football field. All he thought about was making it to the professional league. He had not considered a career other than that. The professional football players visiting his school spoke about the importance of going to college to get educated. The stories they shared about football players getting injured and then having nothing to fall back on got Michael thinking. Maybe he needed to take his education seriously. He set a goal that he was going to become an academic athlete and begin making good grades a priority. He vowed this would be the first year he would make the honor roll. He set an appointment with his career counselor and checked out tutoring opportunities to start making a real effort at being prepared for college instead of only relying on his athletic abilities.

Goal 3: Healthy Relationships

Relationships can make you or break you. Ask any adult. This is one of the most overlooked areas of personal success or failure in life. Unhealthy relationships steer you away from your dreams and goals and destroy your focus. I remember a quotation I learned in high school while on the speech team. *"No man is an island unto himself." (John Donne, poet)* This means we are not supposed to live only for ourselves. Our lives and personal progress are connected to other people. **Healthy relationships are the connection and association with individuals and organizations that promote quality interaction and provide life-affirming, supportive assistance toward personal and professional growth and achievement.**

Who in your life believes in and supports you? Who adds value to your life? Parents. Siblings. Relatives. Friends. Teachers. Coaches. Pastors. Supervisors. There are all kinds of relationships. Make sure you tell these valuable people over and over how much you appreciate them. Understand the purpose of why they are in your life. Your success is tied to them. I am speaking about people who fit the definition. Not everyone connected to you might be providing "quality interaction" or supporting your future achievements. **If your relationships are not helping you "win," then why are they there?** Ask yourself this question about everyone in your life. Make sure you pay attention to the people around you. We navigate relationships the same way we navigate other life choices. Hang with people that strengthen not weaken you. Make this a priority for the rest of your life. You do not win by yourself or just for yourself. You win through building and maintaining valuable relationships.

D2W Character Scenario

Melanie took her friend's advice and shared with her mother that she was experiencing depression and anxiety over her relationship with her boyfriend Michael. Her mother helped set an appointment with a counselor. She started seeing a counselor weekly to talk about her problems. Melanie set some goals and started journaling her thoughts daily and writing down her feelings to combat anxiety. She also set a goal to find a teenage support group to learn strategies on building self-esteem and confidence. Every time she said something negative about herself she would challenge herself to restate her words and say something positive. She even opened up and started talking about her parent's divorce and how this affected her relationship with Michael to her counselor.

Goal 4: Health/Nutrition/Fitness

Are you health-conscious? Do you eat nutritious meals and exercise regularly? Are you at a healthy weight or overweight? Being healthy is another important area to win in life. **Health/Nutrition/Fitness is a lifestyle that demonstrates one's commitment to responsible health practices, good nutrition, and exercise.** Your physical and mental health is a factor in your ability to meet the challenges of accomplishing your dreams and goals. This does not mean you cannot have health challenges before you succeed. I am sharing that a commitment to healthy lifestyles gives you a winning edge. You have more energy. You feel and look your best. How hard do you think it is for someone who is severely overweight to shop for a suit for a job interview? How much more effort would a person with emphysema due

to smoking need to run the 440 relay? How difficult is it to stay motivated and finish your work when you are depressed? The physical and mental challenges endured by unhealthy people make accomplishing dreams even harder than it is already. **You have to develop healthy habits now. Eat well. Exercise. De-stress your mind and body.** Realize the impact a healthy lifestyle has on your life. Committing to your health must be a part of your value system. Make health a priority, regardless of what others around you are doing.

D2W Character Scenario

After visiting the doctor, Antonio was upset that he had not lost the 20lbs. he wanted to lose. He had not worked out with his trainer for three weeks. He was tired of the jokes about being overweight. He was even more tired of starting to eat healthily and exercising and then quitting. He shared his frustration with Janice about how hard it was to be diligent around his family. Together, they agreed to encourage each other and stick to their health goals. Both of them wanted to lose 20lbs. in the next ten weeks. They set a goal to work out at the gym three times per week. They also committed to start packing their lunch instead of eating at fast food places every day. After ten weeks, Antonio had lost 25lbs. and Janice lost 15lbs. They were proud of their results and vowed to continue.

Goal 5: Financial Education/Responsibility

You can be naïve and wait until you are an adult to think or even consider how important financial education is or you can be mature and realize that successful people know how to use money responsibly and set up their financial lives. Do you have a bank account, savings plan, or investment account? How much money have you ever held in your hand? How much money have you ever earned yourself? It is essential for young people to go through financial literacy training. It is also important for young people to earn money now and demonstrate they know how to responsibly manage money.

Financial education/responsibility is the commitment to building financial knowledge and demonstrating how to utilize money responsibly to finance personal vision and build a secure economic future. Is this one of your goals for yourself? Goal 5 is crucial if you want to experience the life you want instead of a life plagued with a lack of money and stress over finances. Is it easier to stay focused on your dreams when you have the money it takes to pursue your dreams or is it harder to stay focused when you are struggling to pay your rent, cell phone, and buy tires for your car? When you do not have money in your pocket or bank account, you are distracted from pursuing your goals because you are focused on paying for your basic needs.

What is money? Money is simply a resource you exchange for the things you need or want. You need money for a bus pass to get to school or work. You need money to buy your yearbook. Do you want to go to college? You will have to pay for it or at least somebody will. Everywhere you turn, there is always something you need that costs money. Money should not be the goal or the controlling desire. Your dreams and goals should be the desired object, and it takes money to accomplish most goals. Mismanaging your money can slow down or

delay you from accomplishing your dreams and goals. Being able to manage and control your desires for things is paramount to setting up a secure economic future. Young people get into trouble when they are unwilling to save their money and hastily buy things with credit cards. Some adults struggle with this at times. I like what Oprah Winfrey said about managing your desires. *"You can have it all; you just cannot have it all right now."*

If I give you $100 without you having to do anything, how much will you value it? If you had to devote 5 or 10 hours to earn $100, would you value it more? Your choices about money expose your values. When you give your best effort, you think twice about trashing something or not taking care of it. This is why it is life-changing for young people to earn their own money and buy important things they want. You want a car. Save up for the car you want or at least contribute something where it took effort on your part. You want an expensive prom dress that costs $250. It will not hurt you if you help your parents pay for it. These essential experiences reinforce your values. Books and parental lectures cannot give this to you. You have to decide you will commit to this goal. It is time you learn how to make money, use money, and manage money.

D2W Character Scenario

Greg needed to find a summer job to save his last $1,000 for his car. He set a goal to save at least $1,500 in the next four months. He had already saved $2,500. His dad was proud of his self-reliance and mature attitude. Right before school started, Greg and his dad started searching for used cars.

Goal 6: Community Involvement

Remember the quote *"No man is an island to himself,"* shared earlier for Goal 3, dealing with relationships? A community is comprised of many relationships and social groups. You will be more successful when you connect with others, use community resources to further your progress, and contribute your talents to community efforts. **Community involvement is the commitment to being knowledgeable about community needs, resources, and projects as well as being involved in increasing skills, providing assistance, and building relationships.** A fundamental way of getting in position for opportunities is building relationships with people in your community. You cannot stay disconnected and unaware. This leads to frustration because your dreams and goals are connected to others. You need them, and they need you.

If you are not involved in school clubs, community sports, or other organized activities, how will you meet the people connected to your future? If you simply hang around and do not do anything with your free time, you will not have the resources and the relationships in place when you need them. When it comes time to fill out your resume and submit scholarship applications, you will not have any extracurricular activities to list on the document.

Research community resources and determine how they connect to fulfilling your dreams. College counselors. Scholarships. Internships. Mentoring programs. Community parks and recreation centers. Are there some youth programs and resources you can find to help you develop yourself? Are there some people you need to meet who will help guide you with your goals? By staying involved with valuable organizations, people will get to know you. When other influential people know about your interests, abilities, and goals, they are able to inform and connect you with opportunities. This might be an internship, scholarship, and job. Your opportunities are linked to your knowledge, interaction, and the pursuit of community resources.

The other side of community involvement is your need to give back to your community. **It is not just what you get, but also what you give.** Volunteering, tutoring, and working as an intern are examples of contributing in your community. Your community activities can be put on your resume to document skills and experiences. <u>If you have not volunteered in the last three months, find a worthy cause, and build up your hours.</u> Do you want to be a veterinarian? Go volunteer at a pet hospital or animal shelter. Do you need to build your confidence and skills in public speaking? Go volunteer at a community clinic where you

give information to the public. Do you want to build your computer skills? Go work on some administration and computer projects for a community organization. **Whatever you need to strengthen in your resume (Three Highways of Learning: Knowledge, Skills, and Experience), find a community opportunity to fulfill that need.** <u>You will find that, when you give your talents, you will receive more than you expected</u>. Find community resources and get information on how you can get involved. Seek out what you need. Give what you have.

D2W Character Scenario

Eliza spoke to her career mentor and set a goal that she would research the news broadcasting career and seek out an internship in the next three months before her senior year. She was articulate and interested in creative writing. She continuously listened to podcasts addressing social and political issues. She started a blog for her school yearbook club about youth issues in her community. Her teacher was so impressed with her writing that she recommended she attend the youth journalism conference. It cost $500 for a two-week program. Eliza really wanted to attend, but she would have to raise the money. She told Greg and Antonio about the opportunity, and together they set a goal to help her raise the money in one month. They created a school competition event for the best social-conscious writers and rappers. They raised $800. Eliza was able to attend the conference as a representative for her school. While at the conference, Eliza met a new friend two years older who interned at the community public broadcasting station. Eliza learned so much from this experience. She was so excited to learn more about the new broadcasting industry.

Here is a final word on goal-setting. **Set goals that are aligned to your dreams. Remember the structure: DREAMS-GOALS.** Take the challenge. Stretch yourself to accomplish things you can be proud of. Don't always take the easy road. Challenge your mountains. You can do it. You can make it. Get up and move forward.

D2W Stop Sign Alert

Set goals that are aligned to your dreams and supported by your values. Write out your S-M-A-R-T goals and review them daily. Develop a list of individual actions that lead you to the finish line. This will help you set your focus and efforts on what is important. Share them with the important people in your life.

D2W Assignment: It's Your Turn

Develop a SMART goal for each of the six goal areas. Indicate if each goal follows the S-M-A-R-T criteria with a 'Yes' or 'No.'

GOAL 1: PERSONAL DEVELOPMENT   SMART GOAL: _____ S-M-A-R-T (Yes or No) _____

GOAL 2: EDUCATION (Higher Learning)   SMART GOAL: _____ S-M-A-R-T (Yes or No) _____

GOAL 3: HEALTHY RELATIONSHIPS   SMART GOAL: _____ S-M-A-R-T (Yes or No) _____

GOAL 4: HEALTH/ NUTRITION/FITNESS   SMART GOAL: _____ S-M-A-R-T (Yes or No) _____

GOAL 5: FINANCIAL EDUCATION/RESP.   SMART GOAL: _____ S-M-A-R-T (Yes or No) _____

GOAL 6: COMMUNITY INVOLVEMENT   SMART GOAL: _____ S-M-A-R-T (Yes or No) _____

Lesson 12: Tool 3 - Decision-Making

Everyone makes decisions. Not everyone is great at making the right decision or choices, but we all do it every day. What shirt will I wear? Will I wear the blue or brown one? What sport do I want to play this year? Will I try out for the baseball, basketball, or football team? What colleges will I apply for? Do I want a part-time job at the mall or do I work at the family business? You probably make more than 10,000 decisions every year. There are all kinds of decisions to make. Some are easy, and some are tough. Regardless, making decisions is a part of life and a test of your maturity level. **Tool 3 is about decision-making. Decision-making is the act of deciding what you will do to produce a desired result.** The best way to create success for yourself is to make decisions that are consistent with your goals.

If you make a decision to get into a top university or college, then you need to make good grades and study diligently for your tests. If you decide to try out for the varsity football team or the cheerleading squad, you need to practice and prepare yourself. If you decide to get healthy, you need to consistently follow your nutrition and fitness regimen. <u>Your goals determine your decisions, and your decisions determine your actions</u>. Decisions cannot stand by themselves. They must be supported with diligent actions. Your decisions and actions pull you closer or further away from your dreams. There is no need to make decisions if you do not back them with consistent actions.

Are you serious about your goals to make decisions that move you forward, not backward? Remember the 'Put It in Gear' lesson? We are talking about being in the right gear (**Park, Reverse, Neutral, Drive**). If you are serious, then why have you 'parked' your educational goals? What are you doing in 'reverse' going the opposite way if you are trying to build good relationships? Put your life in 'drive' and make decisions that will benefit you.

Life rewards decision-makers. Sometimes you are so unsure about which decision to make that you put off making a decision. *"In any moment of decision the best thing you can do is the right thing, the next best thing is the wrong thing, and the worst thing you can do is nothing."* (**Theodore Roosevelt, the 26th president**) Being indecisive is not a good place to stay for long. This is similar to staying in the 'neutral' gear too long and having Life honk at you to get moving. Sometimes we make the wrong decisions, but at least we can learn from it instead of being paralyzed by fear and indecision. Wrong decisions can be corrected and repaired with better decisions.

As you make decisions, you move your life forward. Make wise decisions and get to the next position on the road. Mature people make decisions consistent with their goals. Your goals will dictate your decisions. A person without goals is not challenged to make wise decisions because they have not defined where they are going. <u>You cannot win in life without making decisions</u>. If you want to be a better ballet dancer like D2W Character Janice, then you might have to make a decision to save your money to enroll in the best dance studio instead of going on the spring vacation trip with friends. If you had to make the decision on either opportunity, then you would choose the one most important to you. **Priorities are determined by what is most important.** You cannot do everything. The first step is to make up your mind. The next step is doing the work. Decision-makers should be encouraged because success and support comes when you have strong determination. *"Once you make a decision, the universe conspires to make it happen." (Ralph Waldo Emerson, poet)*

D2W Character Scenario

Everyone seemed to know what they were going to do with their life after high school graduation. They had real passion for their dreams and goals. Michael made a decision to take the full-ride football scholarship. Janice decided she would pursue her dream to dance and move to New York with her aunt and attend the University of Arts Dance Academy. Melanie was the only one undecided and confused about what she would do with her life. Her parents drilled into her that she needed to do well in school and figure out what she was going to do. She was tired of her friends saying she was privileged just because her family could pay for any university. She was confused just thinking about the decisions she needed to make. She made an appointment to speak with her career guidance counselor.

D2W Stop Sign Alert

Make decisions that are aligned with your goals. Take action to prove you are committed. Do not be indecisive. Get the information and guidance you need. It is better for you to move forward by making a decision than to procrastinate and waver back and forth. As you begin making quality decisions even in the smallest way, you will see how each decision connects to the next one and moves you down the road.

D2W Assignment: It's Your Turn

Review your six goals from Lesson 11. Identify the 'gear' that you are in currently for each goal. Identify your actions by completing the 'I have decided' sentences.

GOAL 1: PERSONAL DEVELOPMENT   GEAR: _____   I have decided to _____

GOAL 2: EDUCATION (Higher Learning)   GEAR: _____   I have decided to _____

GOAL 3: HEALTHY RELATIONSHIPS   GEAR: _____   I have decided to _____

GOAL 4: HEALTH, NUTRITION, & FIT.   GEAR: _____   I have decided to _____

GOAL 5: FINANCIAL EDUCATION/RESP.   GEAR: _____   I have decided to _____

GOAL 6: COMMUNITY INVOLVEMENT   GEAR: _____   I have decided to _____

Lesson 13: Responding to the Road Signs of Life

When you are driving, look out the window and notice how many road signs you can find. There are road signs displaying **Stop, Wrong Turn, Do Not Enter, U-Turn, 55 MPH,** and many others. Road signs do three things for us. **They inform, regulate, and warn.**

The purpose of road signs is to assist your driving experience, not to make it more difficult. **Life also gives you road signs to help improve your decision-making.** It might take the form of another person providing guidance or their opinion. It also might be someone sharing their past experiences as a warning for you to consider the consequences. There is no use getting mad at the road signs Life gives you. There is a lesson in everything you go through if you look for it, meaning that there is a purpose for all things. Be diligent to find the answers.

When you spot one of Life's road signs, identify its purpose. If you do not pay attention to the road signs, you might make costly decisions and mistakes that could have been avoided. I am sure there are some people you might know right now who wish they could go back and listen to the advice they were given before they made the worst decisions in their life. *Quitting college. Quitting a musical instrument. Ditching school. Committing a crime.* The decisions are endless. Some decisions do not have a big impact, but others can be life-changing. Life will look out for you and present road signs, but you have to listen. Do your part. Be aware and diligent to respond appropriately. Be ready to listen and make the best decisions once you have the information. The rest will be provided. Below are three

D2W character scenarios to demonstrate when Life is providing signs to <u>inform</u>, <u>regulate</u>, and <u>warn</u> you.

D2W Character Scenario

INFORMATION ROAD SIGN: Greg's dad shared how important it was for the auto mechanic to check out the used car Greg wanted to buy. The auto mechanic was late for the appointment. Greg was impatient and did not want to listen or wait any longer. He wanted to buy his car now. He had saved up $3,500 and he was tired of waiting. Summer was almost over, and he wanted a car before his senior year began. It was 2pm. Greg would have to reschedule his appointment.

What would you do in this example? Would you listen to your dad's advice or make a premature decision? **This is an example of an "informational" road sign.** You have had these encounters. Other people have tried to wisely inform you. It could be the voice of your parents or guardians. *A teacher. An older brother or sister. A friend.* Did you listen to their words or reject them? Did you say to them or yourself, *"I am old enough to make my own decisions?"* You are right that a sign of maturity is for you to take responsibility for your own decisions, but get advice, weigh it out, and make an informed decision. Learning to make your own decisions is what growing up is all about; however, it does not mean you do not look for other influences to guide you as you make decisions for your life.

The next D2W character scenario is a road sign indicating the need to regulate behavior. Have you noticed "No U-Turn" or "Merge" road signs? These road signs go beyond informing; they guide or restrict movement. So many young people today are tempted to toss out or underestimate the value of what their parents or older adults may share with them. We need wisdom and guidance from others to choose the best path. Do not get an attitude when people in authority give you instructions to help you make better decisions and steer you away from harm. Be thankful and appreciate that these people want to help you. **Most adults are not trying to control you. They are trying to get you to be mature enough to control yourself.** Controlling you is not the prize. The goal is for you to be in "the driver's seat."

They simply want the best for you, and if you are wise, you will value their presence in your life and seek them out for counsel or guidance. Instead of thinking they are out to ruin your fun and getting an attitude and not listening, find out what information is being shared and how you can use it to win in life.

D2W Character Scenario

REGULATE ROAD SIGN. Michael and the other football team members listened to the coach share about keeping their grades up to prevent academic probation. All the players had to maintain a 2.0 GPA, but Michael's dad insisted that he maintain a 3.5 GPA to stay on the team. He thought this was unfair and was struggling in his English and Trigonometry classes. Right before the big game, the top quarterback was benched and placed on academic probation. Michael did not want this to happen to him. After his progress report card showed his grades slipping, he made an appointment with his academic counselor to find a tutor. He had a long conversation with his dad about his priorities.

Do you believe it is unfair for Michael to be restricted from playing on the football team if his grades slip? What do you believe about Michael's dad regulating his involvement and expecting higher results? Wise people seek to understand the purpose of the road signs and the consequences, if they do not heed them. They regulate or check their behavior and find a way to make their best decisions.

The last D2W character scenario involves a warning road sign. These road signs usually have red writing or flashing lights. Life tries to warn us. Have you seen Wrong Way, Do Not Enter, and Caution signs? The purpose of warning road signs is to save your life. The purpose of these warning road signs is to get your attention before you make critical decisions. Realize that there are decisions that can end your life or alter it in a major way. Stop taking life for granted just because you are young. People's lives are ending right now because they are not responding to Life's road signs in a responsible way. It's that serious!!!

'DO NOT ENTER' ROAD SIGN. *Melanie was so jealous and insecure about the other cheerleaders always flirting with Michael during and after football practice. She did not know what to do to control her boyfriend. This weekend her parents were out of town, and they trusted her to be responsible and stay at home. This was her chance to make an impression on Michael so he would not turn to anyone else. She decided to throw a party at her house when her parents were out of town. Her best friend Janice thought it was a horrible idea and it would just backfire. She warned her not to do it, but Melanie did not listen. Melanie stole her older sister's ID and bought some alcoholic drinks. Everything was turning out just as she planned until she got into an argument with Michael and the police came to her residence responding to the loud noise complaints, and saw underage drinking. The police shut down the party, and her parents had to come home immediately. The police warned Melanie and her parents about the consequences of underage drinking. Her parents were so disappointed and placed her on restriction for weeks.*

If this happened to you, would you be upset at yourself that you did not follow Janice's warning? Do you believe Melanie got what she wanted? In this D2W character scenario, Melanie is insecure and manipulating situations to get what she believes she wants. The outcome might not have been life-altering, but what if someone was killed after drinking alcohol? Decision-making is the foundation of maturity. You have to own up to your decisions. When you make bad or careless decisions, you need to feel the real impact of the decision. Hopefully, parents and other good-intentioned people are not saving you from your mistakes. You will never learn how to manage your life if you cannot fully feel the impact of your decisions. Young people who are short-changed or bailed out from the outcomes of their wrong actions are simply being preserved for greater catastrophes later. You cannot be carried for the rest of your life. It is time to stand up and realize you are in training to be a responsible adult. You are not always going to get it right. That is okay. You are human, but learn to respond to Life's road signs.

D2W Stop Sign Alert

Show respect and heed the road signs. Do not act as though you know everything and nothing bad can happen to you. The purpose of road signs is to provide information, guidance, or warning. If heeded, road signs will help you to keep moving in a positive direction. If not heeded, you will be responsible for the consequences. Figure out the significance of road signs and respond in a timely manner. In life, road signs usually start with information, but irresponsible drivers wait until they are warned.

D2W Assignment: It's Your Turn

Pick three decisions you are currently considering and recognize an appropriate road sign in your life that could guide your decision. (One-way, No U-turn, Do not enter, etc.)

Identify the purpose of the road sign. (Inform, regulate, or warn)

Decision: _____ Road Sign: _____ Purpose: _____

Decision: _____ Road Sign: _____ Purpose: _____

Decision: _____ Road Sign: _____ Purpose: _____

Lesson 14: Plan the Course of Your Life

Your decisions create the life you will live. Your life starts taking shape as you make decisions. In essence, your decisions should create a course leading you where you want to be. Once you fill out the DREAM Clouds (What do I want to BE? What do I want to HAVE? What do I want to EXPERIENCE?) and answer the three questions (Where am I now? Where am I Going? What do I need to get there?), you can start the planning process. This is where you start moving and separating from those around you who have chosen different paths. You meet new people traveling on the same roads you are traveling on. Your friends now may not be the friends on your future path. The decisions they will make might not be on the course you will create for yourself. This is normal. Get ready for this and do not panic.

Here's an assignment: Ask several adults what kind of decisions they were making when they were your age. Next, ask them what type of decisions they were making during their 20s, 30s, and 40s. Understand the significance and impact of the decisions from the different age groups. You will discover that, as you get older, your decisions become more involved. Your decisions in high school might involve what elective courses to take or what school clubs you want to be involved in. However, as you mature, some decisions involve what career or business industry you want to pursue. Some decisions influence your relationships and will affect you for the rest of your life. **Watch out for the decisions that have the potential to define and shape your life for 5, 10, or more years. The decisions you make today can affect you for decades.** Life-altering decisions should not be taken lightly. Remember, every decision we make is not always the best one, but the trick is to stay encouraged, set your goals, and make decisions that are consistent with where your dreams are leading you.

MAKE A DECISION. Today you make a decision to go to college. You make a decision on which scholarships to apply for. You made a decision to apply for colleges and universities on the East Coast. You decide to accept your first job after college in your hometown. You meet a serious person and decide to spend the rest of your life with that person. You decide to start a family. **Your life is formed. Your course is set. Your life is a result of your personal decisions.**

YOU NEED A PLAN. Life is to be planned. After you make a decision, now it is time for you to make a plan. Anytime you have a dream, a goal, and make a decision, you will need to create a plan of action. Did you get that? **A decision without a plan is simply a good intention or a good thought.** This means the life that you will live is the life you will plan. If you decided to go to college, then create a plan to study for the SAT Test. If you decided to apply for scholarships, then create a plan to apply for five scholarships every three months. If you decided to go to college on the East Coast, create a plan to research East Coast colleges and submit college applications. The decisions and plans you make right now will create the life you will live tomorrow.

<u>The decisions you made yesterday created the life you are living right now.</u>

If you don't like your life, change your decisions. You are that powerful.

D2W Character Scenario

Janice and Melanie were best friends. They had grown up taking ballet classes together since they were five years old. Janice continued with ballet, and her dream was to be a professional dancer. She really wanted to expand her performance resume and be a lead ballet dancer at the spring ballet recital. Melanie was not serious and quit ballet once she was in high school. She was not passionate about anything specific like Janice and was not sure what school clubs or extracurricular activities she wanted to be involved in during her high school years. She considered cheerleading, ASB club, and the drama club, but she was not sure.

Since Janice made the decision to be a professional ballet dancer, her next step is to set some goals and create a plan detailing the actions needed to be successful. Melanie was unsure about her decisions, so her next step is to research and meet people in the different school clubs.

ACTION PLAN

An action plan lists out the individual actions, the people involved, and the timeframe of completing actions.

Janice's action plan:

Research best ballet dance schools – Janice, 11th-grade year

Find a mentor – Janice & counselor, 11th-grade year

Enroll and pay for summer ballet camp, Janice & Mom, Summer months

Apply for part-time job - Janice, 12th grade

Audition for spring ballet recital to build resume – Janice, Spring months

Melanie's action plan:

Research the schedules of different school clubs – Melanie, 11th grade, Fall months

Go visit each club meeting and meet leaders – Melanie, 11th grade, Fall months

Find out the open positions in the school clubs – Melanie, 11th grade, Fall months

PROJECT ACTION PLAN

A project plan is a detailed plan listing multiple related actions, the people responsible for each task, the timeframe of completing actions, and costs associated with each task.

Janice's Project Action Plan: Compete in spring ballet recital

Find dance partner – October

Enter competition and pay entry fee – October - $100

Finish choreographing dance routine – November

Buy costumes – November - $250

Get hair and makeup done – December - $200

Take pictures – December - $150

Compete in ballet competition - December

Melanie's Project Action Plan: Join the cheerleading squad and try out for captain

Go to school club meetings – Melanie, September

Decide on school club to join – Melanie, Mid-October

Prepare cheerleader tryout routine – Melanie & dance coach, November, $250

Try out for Cheerleader Captain Position – Melanie, November

The action plan and the project action plan are similar planning tools. Both action plans list actions, people involved, and the timeframe of the activities. The main difference between them is that the project action plan is more comprehensive. The project action plan helps you stay organized when you have a detailed project with related activities, schedule, and associated costs.

CONTINGENCY PLAN

A contingency plan is a plan identifying the actions you will take to find solutions to problems if your initial plan is not successful.

Sometimes plans do not work out the way you want. Even the best plans do not work out exactly as expected. Maybe Janice's ballet partner gets sick, or she does not have enough money for the costumes. Maybe the date for the competition is changed and moved up a week earlier, so now she has to hurry to finalize the choreographed dance.

These circumstances are made up, but in real life when things do not work out as planned, we experience problems. You have to anticipate that 100% of your plans will not go as you wanted them to. What do you do? **You have to adjust and make other arrangements and new actions to get your overall goal accomplished.** This is where you will need a contingency plan. This is a big word, but it simply means planning actions you will take if your first plan does not succeed. **The DREAM and GOAL stay the same, but the PLAN of ACTION may have to change. Remember the structure: Build a DREAM, Set a GOAL, Make wise DECISIONS and Take responsible ACTIONS.**

If the D2W character Janice's ballet partner got sick and could not be involved any longer, what would she do? Give up? Find a new partner? How long would it take and how soon could he learn the dance routine before the competition date? These considerations are necessary to keep moving toward the overall goal. The contingency plan details actions to get back on track and overcome the unexpected circumstances, which threatened the plan.

Janice's contingency plan:

Ask community ballet teacher to recommend a new ballet partner.

Put out a social media request for a new ballet partner.

Revise practice session to three times per week instead of two times per week.

Resize costume.

Janice was discouraged that her dance partner got ill. They had worked so diligently for three weeks. They had paid their entry fees and just picked out their music and dance costumes. She had to make new decisions quickly if she was still going to compete. She decided not to quit. She created a contingency plan and listed all the actions to get the project back on track. She interviewed new dance partners and then started practicing rigorously. After a few weeks, Janice and her new dance partner were ready to compete. They got second in the competition.

If the D2W character Melanie was not picked for the cheerleader captain leader, what other school club opportunities would she pursue?

Melanie's contingency plan:

Try out for ASB Club.

Get a part-time job on the weekends.

Melanie did not get picked for the cheerleading squad for the two open positions, but they told her she could come back next semester and try out again. She was disappointed, but she encouraged herself and decided to try out for the ASB Club leadership and also find a part-time job for the weekends. She kept herself busy and met new friends. She was proud of herself for trying, and she would definitely be ready next semester.

To restate, there are three types of plans. **Action plan. Project Action Plan. Contingency Plan.** Janice had dreams and goals. This gave her a reason to create a plan. The decisions that Janice made created a course filled with actions to complete. Melanie's personal development goals led her to make decisions to find a school club she could be involved in. Her actions led her to prepare for the cheerleading tryouts. When she did not make the team, she had to make an alternate plan to join the ASB Club and get a part-time job. Decision-making is a critical tool to learn when you are young. **People with dreams make decisions. Make decisions and create plans of action.** One good decision after the other creates your life.

D2W Stop Sign Alert

Once you make a decision about where you want to go in life, the next step is to create a plan and determine the coordinating actions. If you do not set goals or make decisions, you will never need a plan. Study successful people who have attained what you want. Ask them what they did to get ahead and what to look out for. Keep your eye on them; they are the ones following a plan and taking action.

D2W Assignment: It's Your Turn

Identify three goals or projects you are involved in that involve several actions.
(Examples: school project, sports team assignment, college planning project.)
Identify which planning tool should be used. (Action plan or Project action plan)
List a situation that might require you to create a contingency plan.

Goal/Project 1: _____ Planning tool: _____ Situation: _____

Goal/Project 2: _____ Planning tool: _____ Situation: _____

Goal/Project 3: _____ Planning tool: _____ Situation: _____

Lesson 15: Tool 4-Problem-Solving/Evaluation

Can you imagine life without problems? That would be great. Nobody wants to face problems, but everyone has to face them at times. Problems are always regarded as negative. However, there are some good things that can come from facing problems. **A problem is defined as a matter or situation involving unpleasant circumstances or difficult choices.** Problems help us to learn something about ourselves. They challenge us to demonstrate strong character and not give up on our dreams. We have the opportunity to find out what does not work and find better solutions to move us closer to attaining our goals. If it wasn't for problems and how bad we feel when we go through them, some people would continue to be immature and irresponsible forever. Also, we sure would not appreciate the good times as much.

Problem-Solving/Evaluation is about simply finding solutions to problems. Evaluation is making an assessment of where you are on the road and what you have obtained. Name some problems you have right now. Do you have a plan to solve them? Every problem does not mean you did something wrong, but when you are at fault, think through the issues and learn what you are doing wrong. **For the problems you named, did you do something wrong?**

---

9 Steps to Problem-Solving

1. Recognize and acknowledge the problem.
2. Identify the symptoms of the problem.
3. Determine the cause of the problem.
4. Assess the impact of the problem.
5. Revisit the 3Q for a successful journey. *(Lesson 2)*
6. Inventory your character. *(Tool 1)*
7. Create goals. *(Tool 2)*
8. Make appropriate decisions and actions. *(Tool 3)*
9. Evaluate results. (Tool *4)*

Did you wait until the last minute and not finish your five-page essay that was due? That could present a problem, especially if you needed a good grade on your paper to avoid academic probation. Sometimes we cause our own problems. Why? Character flaws: Laziness. Procrastination and Forgetfulness. To solve or correct a problem, it takes strong character. You must replace laziness with diligence. You must replace forgetfulness with assertiveness. If you want to win, you cannot quit, but instead, you must be resilient.

When we solve problems, we are moving past roadblocks that obstruct the path to our goals. This includes negative mindsets and behaviors.

There are nine steps to problem-solving. It sounds like a lot, but five of the steps have already been introduced in the D2W lessons. To illustrate, let's identify a problem of one of the D2W characters. The school police searched Greg's locker and found drug paraphernalia in a backpack. Greg is threatened with being expelled from school and facing drug possession charges, but he explains that he was unaware of what was in the bag, and he was holding the bag for a friend. He is ordered to provide the name of the owner of the backpack.

Let's go through the nine steps to problem-solving. **Step 1 is recognizing and acknowledging the problem.** Greg is in trouble for violating the school policy and not being responsible for what is in his possession on the school campus. Is Greg's problem that he is in trouble with his school or is it the unhealthy friendships he maintains? What is the real problem? **It is not always easy identifying the real problem. Unhealthy relationships are the problem.** You cannot pretend the problem does not exist. Be honest and face the truth. **Step 2 is identifying the symptoms of the problem.** The symptoms are what is happening or the situation Greg finds himself in. Symptoms are not the problem, but the evidence that there is a problem. **The symptom is that Greg is worried about facing expulsion from school and criminal charges.**

Step 3 involves determining the cause of the problem. What made this problem happen? His old neighborhood friend asked him to store his backpack in his school locker. Greg knew his friend had questionable behavior, and he suspected he was dealing drugs at school, but Greg was too afraid to question him. He did not say 'No' when his friend asked him to hold his backpack. He was not assertive. The cause of the problem is having a lack of confidence to say 'No' to friends and peer pressure. **Step 4 is about evaluating the impact of the problem. How did this problem impact Greg?** Greg might have to face criminal charges and attend another school. Steps 1-4 are the beginning steps of problem-solving. They are initial steps to understand what is really happening to solve the problem completely.

The next five steps are repeats of the previous D2W lessons. **Step 5 involves the 'Three Questions for a Successful Journey.' (Where am I NOW? Where am I GOING? What do I NEED to get there?)** When you are facing problems, ask these three questions, just as when you are planning the path toward your dreams. Greg wants to graduate on time, be with his friends, and avoid unnecessary problems. *Where is he now?* He is in trouble and about to be expelled from school and face criminal charges. *Where is he going?* He would like to continue attending his school and keep playing basketball with his team. *What does he need to get there?* He needs to maintain positive relationships and be more responsible for his actions.

<u>**Step 6 involves taking inventory of your character, which is Tool 1: Character-building.**</u> This step helps you to take inventory of your character traits. In this scenario, Greg needs to be **diligent** to make some changes. He needs to be **earnest** or sincere about following the school policies. He needs to be **assertive** and share with his friends when he is uncomfortable about their actions. When you are solving problems, revisit the 20 character keys, and figure out which ones need to be demonstrated to get things moving in the right direction.

<u>**Step 7 involves Tool 2: Goal-setting.**</u> As always, connecting with your goals gets you back on track as you solve problems. In Greg's case, a goal could be as simple as maintaining friendships with people consistent with his values and morals.

<u>**Step 8 involves Tool 3: Decision-making.**</u> By making better decisions and taking responsible actions, you move forward. Greg's decision to hold a backpack for a friend expected of selling drugs was the wrong decision. A new decision for Greg could be to stop hanging out with friends doing things that can get him into a lot of trouble. <u>Do not continue to make the decisions that created the problem</u>. Make new decisions. Should Greg share the name of his friend or be expelled from school? That will be his choice, but a real friend wants you to be successful. They care about you and do not want to get you in trouble or harm you.

<u>**The last step is Step 9, which is Tool 4: Problem-Solving/Evaluation**</u>. This step involves using the five controls from the 'Control Panel' to evaluate whether the problem is solved and results are improved. Step 9 also involves evaluating the results of behavior and decisions. Greg shared that he was unaware of the contents of the backpack to the school officials. He persuaded his friend to confess it was his backpack. He understood his role in the matter and made a commitment to his parents he would be more careful of his actions and make better decisions with his friendships.

All of the steps in the nine-step process are necessary. Each step is important in understanding how to solve problems thoroughly. The more involved the problem, the more you will have to consciously go through each step carefully. For easier problems, you can breeze through the nine steps without much effort. Identify the real problem, the symptom, causes, and impact. Answer the Three Questions for a Successful Journey. Revisit the four 'Tools of Life.' All these steps help you to solve your problems and keep your life on track. **"*You don't drown by falling in the water; you drown by staying there.*"** *(Edwin Louis Cole)* Problems do not last forever. Do not be overwhelmed. <u>Your dreams and goals are bigger than your problems</u>. Find your strength. Encourage yourself and move beyond your current setbacks.

D2W Stop Sign Alert

Problems come and go. If you are smart, you will search out what you can learn from the experience so you will be stronger. However, if you have problems because you have more goals or you take more risk than others, do not worry. Life has a way of rewarding the risk-takers for their courage and endurance.

D2W Assignment: It's Your Turn

List three problems you have encountered and the character strengths needed to overcome them. Identify any lessons learned and any causes for the problem.

Problem #1: _____ Character Key: _____ Lesson Learned/Causes: _____

Problem #2: _____ Character Key: _____ Lesson Learned/Causes: _____

Problem #3: _____ Character Key: _____ Lesson Learned/Causes: _____

Lesson 16: What to Do in Bad-Weather Situations

"When it rains, it pours." Have you heard that saying? Have you ever been doing just fine and in a good mood, nothing was bothering you, and then you get a phone call about something that just happened all of a sudden? *"Why did this have to happen to me? Why now? Everything was going so well."* We call these unexpected experiences "bad-weather problems." We all have them. **Bad-weather situations are those experiences that come to your life, and you do not expect them.** These experiences come all of a sudden, without any warning, and they are not necessarily anyone's fault. They just happen. Think about driving and getting stuck in a flood or powerful winds blowing your car all over the road and causing you to almost lose control. That is what "bad-weather experiences" are like.

They challenge your ability to cope with life and stay focused on your goals. Bad-weather situations challenge you to quit and fall apart.

D2W Character Scenario

Janice was so excited about the ballet camp that she talked about it with her friends for weeks. She would have the opportunity to learn from the best dance instructors from around the world, and she would meet new dancers. The ballet camp costs $1,500. Her mom said she would make the final payment of $600 in the next two weeks. Unfortunately, Janice's mom learned that her company was laying off employees due to business slowdowns and she would not have a job in two weeks. Her mom knew that it would be a struggle to pay for the ballet camp and keep the bills current while looking for a new job.

This is a "bad-weather experience." **Can you see how this was not Janice's fault?** She did not do anything to cause this problem. This did not happen because she demonstrated character weaknesses like forgetfulness, laziness, or impatience. In fact, she did everything right. When this happens, the only thing to do is stay encouraged, stay focused on your goals, and start making plans to solve your problems. **So, what would you do if you were Janice?** Would you understand that your family needed help right now and give up on the camp? Would you yell and scream and say life is not fair? Would you be selfish and have an attitude at your mom and insist that she find a way to pay? Life has a way of presenting problems to you unexpectedly and testing your character to see if you will crumble and fall or rise and stand. Let's see what Janice did to win in this situation.

D2W Character Scenario

Instead of staying discouraged Janice went to her ballet teacher and shared how she needed to earn the money to make the last $600 payment. To her surprise, her ballet teacher had recently lost her ballet assistant and needed some assistance with the upcoming community ballet recital for the toddlers. With this new weekend job and some donations from dance studios she had volunteered at, Janice persisted with her goals and found a way to pay the remaining ballet camp fees.

Bad-weather problems are not always about money. They could be about personal sickness, family problems, or other experiences you do not expect. You might be tempted to ask, *"Why me? What did I do to deserve this?"* That is a waste of time. The best thing you can do is become a person with strong determination, build relationships with caring people who will encourage you, and do not give up when problems test you. Problems challenge you to build inner strength and be resilient. <u>What you are building on the inside has to be larger than what challenges you on the outside.</u> <u>See problems as a tool to make you stronger by serving your future.</u> It's hard, I know. Focus on the mountaintop, not the mountain. Visualize where you are going. Do not lose heart. Remember the last problems in your life? How long did they last? How were they solved? Problems are not bigger than you. Problems are external, but your strength is internal. Keep it together and know that problems are like clouds. They move in; they fizz out. The real you is what lasts. Keep it moving. Win big.

D2W Stop Sign Alert

Do not be surprised when bad-weather experiences come. Expect them to show up at different times in your life. Do not be overwhelmed. That is a part of life and the learning process. Keep looking beyond your struggles to your future. Speak to anyone who has succeeded; they all had tough times. Tough times do not last, but tough people do. Your hard work will pay off. Endure to the end and keep driving down the right roads. You will get to your bright and positive future. The journey continues no matter the struggle.

D2W Assignment: It's Your Turn

List three 'bad weather' problems you have encountered that were not a result of bad behavior or wrong choices. What character strengths did you demonstrate to overcome them?

Problem #1: _____   Character Key: _____

Problem #2: _____   Character Key: _____

Problem #3: _____   Character Key: _____

Lesson 17: Preventive Maintenance

We talked about problems you face when you have not done anything to cause them. Now, let's speak about problems that you create as a result of your flawed character and bad decisions. These are problems that could be avoided altogether if preventive measures were taken. **Preventive maintenance is the work you do on your life before it breaks down from lack of care or misbehavior.** Do you know anyone facing tough problems right now and regretting the decisions they made? Do you know anyone your age or a little older who is flunking out of school, in jail or detention center, addicted to drugs, or facing pregnancy as a teenager? What about you? What are you dealing with? Do you have some big problems that you created by the decisions you made? Maybe your problems are not that serious, but what about being grounded or in trouble because of lying, stealing, fighting, or something else? Do you believe these problems could have been avoided given a different set of behaviors or decisions?

We open the door to unnecessary problems by our decisions. Let's look at some situations. You are good at Algebra, and you normally do well in this subject. If you fail the test because you were not paying attention during your teacher's lecture, who is at fault? If you stayed up all night, did not set your alarm, and missed the bus to the basketball championship game out of town, who is at fault? If you ditched school with friends continually, failed a few classes, and now have to attend summer school, who is at fault? Do you see how these problems are home-grown? Nobody twisted your arm and made you do it. These problems are preventable. In these examples, choices are being made, and character keys are unlocking negative certain situations.

When you develop good character, set goals, and make good decisions, you protect yourself from creating unnecessary problems. This is preventive maintenance for your life. 'Checking under the Hood' and taking the VIPC assessment is an example of preventive maintenance. This is characteristic of Step 6 of the problem-solving model (Inventory your character). You make better decisions when you are aware of your values and interests.

When you have interests and goals that are important to you, you think twice before doing stupid things. You count the cost and realize the impact of your decisions and behavior. You do not want to create roadblocks and more problems for yourself. You have too much to lose. Do not complicate your life and waste your time by demonstrating negative character traits. Stay alert. Do not be careless and add more drama to your life.

D2W Character Scenario

Greg didn't realize the mess he created just by holding his friend's backpack in his school locker. He knew there was talk about Lenny selling drugs at school, but that was his friend from the neighborhood. He could not turn his back on him. What was the worst that could happen? No big deal. Lenny would be back in two hours to get his backpack. When the school principal and the school police showed up at Greg's English class asking for him, he had no idea how his world would be turned upside down. Not only did he get caught up and suspected of selling drugs with Lenny, but he had to go to the police station for a lineup for a burglary charge. His car was searched by police dogs, and his seats were scratched up from the police search. He was cleared of all the charges, but he was still angry with Lenny. He was really mad at himself for being so trusting and jeopardizing his reputation.

D2W Stop Sign Alert

Avoid creating unnecessary problems because of a lack of character or wrong decisions. When you mess up, do not waste time staying discouraged. Figure out where you went wrong and what needs to be redirected or changed to get back on track.

D2W Assignment: It's Your Turn

List the three problems from Lesson 15 created as a result of your decisions. Write down the decision(s) made to create the problem. Identify a better decision.

Problem #1: _____   Decision made: _____   Better Decision: _____

Problem #2: _____   Decision made: _____   Better Decision: _____

Problem #3: _____   Decision made: _____   Better Decision: _____

Lesson 18: Using the Control Panel to Solve Life's Problems

Facing problems is not easy, but it is necessary. There are pressures that make life really hard, and it is not always easy to see how best to deal with them. How do you solve your problems and get your life back on track? Problems can really get you down, especially when you do not see a way out. Sometimes you might have to work out issues for weeks, months, or even years before you solve them. Whether it is a 'bad-weather' experience or a problem you created from flawed character and decisions, you have to deal with it. So, what do you do?

Using the control panel is a way to start fixing or solving your problems. Remember the lesson on the control panel? There are five controls: **1) Fuel Gauge - Resources, 2) Speedometer – Time Management, 3) Tachometer - Effort, 4) Temperature Gauge - Attitude, and 5) Odometer - Progress.** It is essential to perform well in all of these areas to accomplish any dream or goal. When you are facing multiple problems, it is frustrating to figure out where to start if you do not know what you are dealing with. If you look at each control panel gauge, you can begin to identify the type of problems you are encountering and take action to solve them.

In this D2W character scenario, Melanie is facing several problems. *Can you relate to what Melanie is experiencing? Do you find yourself dealing with several things at the same time?* **RESOURCES** - Melanie's resource problem is that she spent all her money, has a negative balance at the bank, and cannot pay for her spring vacation trip. **PACE/ TIME MANAGEMENT** – Melanie accepted more hours at work than she could handle with her current priorities. **EFFORT** – Melanie procrastinated and did not study for her SAT Test to be prepared. She is also behind in her Algebra assignments. **ATTITUDE** – Melanie is depressed after learning about her parent's divorce. **PROGRESS** – Melanie has several commitments she has not met.

What should Melanie do to solve her problems? Melanie needs to sort out her problems using the five control panel areas. Sometimes when you are so perplexed about your problems you cannot think clearly. When you are "going through it" or overwhelmed your perspective is compromised. Look at the five control gauges and decide on the appropriate actions for each type of problem area when you are experiencing problems. **RESOURCES** - Melanie will cut back on buying frivolous things at the mall with friends and use her money from her part-time job to fix her bank account and save for her spring vacation trip. **PACE/TIME MANAGEMENT** – Melanie has created a schedule and is working only 20 hours a week at her part-time job. She is going to the tutoring lab to make up her Algebra assignments two days per week. She rescheduled her SAT Exam for next month and signed up for a weekly study group. **EFFORT** – Melanie is now focusing on her commitments and working diligently. **ATTITUDE** – Melanie is not feeling pressured and anxious about life. She is handling her stress better. She is also speaking with her parents and a counselor about the divorce. **PROGRESS** – Melanie is doing much better now that she is working through each problem. These are all proactive steps to solve problems. **You must 'clear the street' so you have a clear vision and path to proceed down the road.**

As your problems are clearing up, there is one last step to take, which is to evaluate whether the steps taken solved the problems. The five controls help you identify your problems, but also provide areas to evaluate if your dreams and goals are on track. Ask yourself these questions: **RESOURCES** - *Do I have the resources needed?* **PACE/TIME MANAGEMENT** – *Am I doing too much? Am I managing my time well?* **EFFORT** – *Am I putting in the adequate amount of effort?* **ATTITUDE** – *Am I experiencing anxiety or stress?* **PROGRESS** – *Am I accomplishing my tasks?* Be honest with your answers. These questions will help you know what problems have been solved and which ones need more work. Be encouraged!!! There is no problem so big that you cannot work through it. You are greater on the inside than any problem or circumstance on the outside. **Be Driven 2 Win. Be D2W.**

<u>D2W Stop Sign Alert</u>

If you cannot communicate what type of problem you are experiencing, then other people cannot help you effectively. Communication is essential to finding answers. Sometimes it is necessary to communicate your problems with trustworthy people. Let them know what you are dealing with. If you can accurately sort and identify what you are going through, you will find answers quicker and keep moving forward.

D2W Assignment: It's Your Turn

Rewrite three problems from any of the previous lessons and evaluate yourself on how well you are at solving your problems in the five control panel areas. (5 Areas: Resources, Pace/Time Management, Effort, Attitude, Progress) (Rating: 1 to 5; 5 being the highest)

Problem #1: _____ Control Panel Area: _____ _____ _____ _____ _____

Problem #2: _____ Control Panel Area: _____ _____ _____ _____ _____

Problem #3: _____ Control Panel Area: _____ _____ _____ _____ _____

Lesson 19: S-W-O-T Your Life

If you look back at the problems you had last year, you are probably not dealing with them anymore. You probably already forgot about them. You are dealing with new problems. Life is filled with problems for many different reasons, as we have seen. As you overcome one problem, here comes another. **Problems present a challenge to your dreams and goals.** You cannot be afraid of problems, no matter how big. You will be afraid to live. One effective tool to problem-solving is S-W-O-T analysis. This is a business term. I am encouraging you to S-W-O-T your life. **The S-W-O-T model is a problem-solving tool that helps you analyze four important factors in your life that can help you gain a better perspective and solve your problems.**

Here is how it works. **'S' stands for Strengths.** Sounds familiar? These are the same character strengths or character keys we have been speaking about. **Figure out what character keys you need to "unlock" to face your challenge.** *Do you need to be diligent?* When you demonstrate the D-R-E-A-M character keys, you are working from the inside out. You are becoming a better, stronger person.

'W' stands for Weaknesses. These are negative character keys that open the doors to more problems. All of us are plagued with negative character keys or behaviors that 'lock and block' us from being successful. We are human. We are not perfect. The best we can do is to minimize these behaviors and reduce their impact. Laziness, dishonesty, inattentiveness, selfishness, and insecurity limit our abilities. Be honest when you fall prey to these behaviors.

Be ready to do inner work to escape these traps. Both 'Strengths' and 'Weaknesses' represent internal character traits or keys that impact our personal success or failure.

For external forces, 'O' stands for Opportunities. Opportunities are always present. They come and go based on our readiness to receive them. If you are wise, you will recognize and take advantage of them. Opportunities stretch us and make us grow as people. You might have a volunteer opportunity to build new skills or an opportunity to be a part of a youth program to meet new people. It takes inner strength to believe in ourselves and pursue new opportunities that challenge our skills and abilities. Do not be afraid to 'take the plunge' when you have prepared yourself. We must break out of our small mindsets to achieve personal power and greatness. It is your time. Let wisdom guide you for every opportunity. Push out fear and doubt. Be brave and do not let opportunities pass you up.

Now, 'T' is for Threats. Nobody wants to face threats. **Threats are major challenges to your life.** They come and go and are external forces like opportunities, but they challenge you to lose your hope or even your life. You might believe that problems and threats are the same things, and sometimes they are. **Threats are perceived as more serious than problems because they can cause personal failure, fear, pain, injury, danger, and harm.** Threats can devastate you. A threat does not mean you necessarily did something wrong or even allowed it to happen. Regardless of the cause, when you face a threat, you need to take it seriously. Examples of threats are major health problems, academic failure, promiscuity/teenage pregnancy, gang violence, family divorce/trauma, crime, depression/mental health challenges, suicide, obesity, drug abuse, and alcoholism.

If we can look past the pain, there is purpose even for threats in our lives, meaning that you have to find a way to use them to make your life better. **You need to realize YOU are greater than any force outside of YOU.** Overcoming threats will definitely take all of your inner strength to stand against the external challenges trying to force your life off the road. Threats are usually not something you can just find the strength and overcome by yourself. You need other people to step in and help you overcome them. This could be as simple as speaking with a counselor or a trustworthy person. Since we know threats will come, especially at times when we do not feel we are ready and do not expect them, the best we can do is acknowledge their presence, remember our problem-solving lessons, "unlock" character strengths or character keys, and access personal power and community support to conquer all challenges.

Using the S-W-O-T model is an effective problem-solving technique because you assess or identify the internal and external forces that are present. Remember, the purpose of this assessment is to solve a problem that stands in the way of your dreams. <u>Identification and inventory starts the process</u>. Go through each letter and determine what is happening, how it is affecting you, and what actions you can take to keep progressing down your personal roads. Take charge of your life.

D2W Stop Sign Alert

Your dreams do not magically become a reality. You have to consciously be focused on creating success for yourself. Life will bring threats and challenges your way, and you will need your character strengths to overcome them. Life will also provide opportunities, but you cannot allow your character weaknesses to trip you up and make you miss what is yours.

D2W Character Scenario

Everyone said Michael had what it took to make it to the top in football. He sensed it also. He put a lot of pressure on himself to help his team win the high school state football championships. He was diligent and a real leader for his team. He worked out to condition himself more than any other player. When failing grades were threatening his game, he buckled down and got serious about his education. He had a real opportunity to get picked for a college scholarship. He was one game away from championship game. He was anxious and kept training a few days before the big game even though his coach told him to rest. Unfortunately, he injured his leg one day before the big game and landed in the hospital. This game was so important for getting noticed by the college scouts. What would happen to his dream for a full-ride college scholarship? Michael was depressed. All his hard work for years seemed meaningless. His big opportunity was gone. How could he recover from this?

D2W Assignment: It's Your Turn

Pick one of your DREAM Clouds or goals. (Refer back to Lesson 1 or Lesson 11.)

Write your dream in the DREAM Cloud. List three strengths or character keys you will need to demonstrate. List three weaknesses you need to control. List three opportunities you will pursue. List three possible threats you might need to overcome.

What do I want to BE?
What do I want to HAVE?
What do I want to EXPERIENCE?

S	W	O	T
Strengths	Weaknesses	Opportunities	Threats
_____	_____	_____	_____
_____	_____	_____	_____
_____	_____	_____	_____

Lesson 20: Life's Intersections: Conflict Resolution

When you are doing things, you know you should not do, your conscience should bother you. If it does not, that is a problem in its own right. When you are doing things opposed to your values and goals, you are at a crossroad. You are at one of Life's intersections. You are in conflict and out of alignment with your commitments. If you present yourself as an honest person, and then you are dishonest, you are in conflict. If you are skipping classes and hanging out instead of studying for tests and you value your education, you are in conflict. If you are flirting with your best friend's boyfriend and you call yourself a good friend, you are at Life's intersection.

Are you living out the values and character strengths to support your goals?

If you commit to certain values and goals, then your decisions and actions need to be aligned. The uneasy feelings you experience when you go against your commitments are signals that you are at an intersection. You are creating conflict and inner turmoil in yourself. Other people may not know you have an internal conflict, but you will know. The uneasiness and guilty feelings are forcing you to make up your mind. You cannot rest in indecision. You will go either left, right or straight. **You must do what it takes to support your goals or give up. You must follow your values or change them.** Most people do not want to change or give up on their values or goals because they are a part of them. It is almost like ripping out your own heart. Once you desire something for your life, you do not want to give up. Even if your current behavior is directly opposed to your commitments, something inside you struggles to do better. If you quit, you give up on yourself. That in itself brings conflict. Again, these experiences are called Life's intersections.

D2W Character Scenario

Antonio was serious this time about losing weight and getting healthy. He diligently worked out with his fitness trainer every week. He was so proud of himself for losing 50lbs. in the last three months by following his nutrition regimen and exercising regularly. The holidays came, and he completely went back to his unhealthy eating even although he had a plan to keep exercising and eating moderately during the holidays. He regained 20lbs. He was disappointed. He overate even more. He was so tired of this vicious cycle.

D2W Character Scenario

Melanie signed up for the SAT Prep Test with her study group. She persuaded her parents to pay $350 for the six-week program. They agreed to pay only if she completed all four training sessions and if she paid for half the program. Melanie had a habit of quitting things and not following through. She vowed it would be different this time. She promised to focus on her goals and not be distracted. She had one more study session to complete this weekend. There was talk that Michael was flirting with the newest cheerleader and he would bring her to the Saturday party. Her SAT Prep study group was meeting so she could not go to the party, anyway. The more she thought about Michael and the other girl she became upset. She was committed to her study group, but she fumed at the situation with Michael. She decided to skip her SAT Prep study group altogether. She spent the money she owed her parents on a new dress and went to the party. When her parents found out, they were disappointed and confronted her about mismanaging her priorities.

Greg was not truthful to his parents when he said he was not speaking or hanging out with Larry. He did not want the guys to know he wasn't down. He knew Larry from the old neighborhood. Even though he went to a new school, that did not mean he could not hang out with them still. He didn't do drugs. He was committed to staying clean for his basketball game. Larry was in a gang, and he wasn't trying to recruit him. What was the harm in hanging out a few times? Michael saw Greg speaking with Larry. Afterward, he questioned him about hanging out and ruining his reputation again. They got into a big argument.

In these D2W character scenarios, the values and goals of the D2W characters are opposed to their behavior. **How do you resolve inner conflict? What do you do when your actions are opposed to your commitments? Check Under the Hood.** Go back to your value system. Figure out why your values are important to who you. **Recommit to your goals.** *Where is your life headed? Is that where you still want to go? What is your motivating reason? Is it still big enough to raise you above your weaknesses and failed experiences?* It is okay to change your mind and move in a different direction if that is what you want. **Make better decisions.** *What decisions are you currently making? Are they the right ones? Are your decisions taking you where you want to go?* **Solve your problems and evaluate your performance.** Identify what type of problems you are experiencing (if any). *Why are they happening? Is there anything you can learn about yourself?*

I know these are a lot of questions, but that is what it takes when you are at Life's intersections. This is a dangerous place. This is where most accidents happen. Remember the 3C's to Personal Disaster: Crashes, Collisions, and Catastrophes? Your life could altogether change based on one decision at one of Life's intersections. **You do not have the option to just sit there and do nothing. Life's intersections force you to make a decision.** You have one life, and you need to get to the end of your destiny. Rev up the engine. Get the D2W Life Management System working for you. Make it automatic. Make it a part of you. It will become second nature and move you into position and out of misalignment and personal conflict.

D2W Stop Sign Alert

You cannot live your life based on what other people value or believe. You must align your behavior and actions to your own value system if you want to stay out of internal conflict. Determine your path and move beyond conflict by being honest about your values, what you want, and what you are willing to do to get it.

D2W Assignment: It's Your Turn

Review each of the six D2W goal areas and definitions. (Refer back to Lesson 11.) Identify whether you value each D2W goal area. Identify if your actions consistently demonstrate that you are committed to each D2W goal area. Identify whether your values and your actions are in conflict or alignment.

	Value? (Y or N)	Committed Actions? (Y or N)	Conflict or Alignment?
Personal Development	————————	————————	————————
Education	————————	————————	————————
Healthy Relationships	————————	————————	————————
Health/Nutrition/Fitness	————————	————————	————————
Financial Education/Resp.	————————	————————	————————
Community Involvement	————————	————————	————————

Final Chapter: Putting it on the Road: Creating Your D2W Roadmap for Personal Success

It's time to create your D2W Roadmap by putting all these lessons on the road. This is a one-page diagram for you to visually map out your dreams, character traits, goals, decisions, and problems as you journey forward. You have been exposed to 20 D2W lessons, which will help you design your D2W Roadmap. If you have read each chapter and then completed the D2W: It's Your Turn assignments, you have all the content material to detail on your own D2W Roadmap. You can refer back to what you have written down. **Prepare a D2W Roadmap daily, weekly, or monthly for each DREAM Cloud to focus your attention on what you are creating for your life**. Make it colorful and personal. Write your name in big letters. Add your favor picture of yourself. Write out your favorite quotes or encouraging statements to 'pump yourself up' for the journey. Add images of your hobbies and interests. You do not have to be an artist, but whatever your style and interest, make it motivational and something that inspires you.

There is a D2W Roadmap for each of the D2W Characters. (See the Appendix files.) Read about their dreams, VIPC profiles, goals, decisions, and problems. Understand how they are using the four 'Tools for Life' to make their dreams a reality. As an example of how the D2W Roadmap works, let's look at D2W Character Janice. **Read her vision statement on what she mentally visualizes outside the windshield for her life**. "I *see myself developing my art, being the lead dancer in several ballet recitals, traveling around the world, and having a successful career.*" **Review her VIPC profile**. She values her faith and family. She is caring, energetic, and fun. She loves dancing and singing. One of her character keys is demonstrating that she is resilient. In the D2W Character scenarios, she demonstrates how she has been resilient to continue dancing regardless of setbacks and disappointments. **Look at her goals**. One of her goals is to learn how to choreograph dances. **Evaluate one of her decisions**. She decides to find a part-time job teaching young kids ballet. **Understand how she solved her financial problems and utilized her resources**. One of her problems was not having enough money for her ballet summer camp. Her part-time job was the answer, but she found that resource by speaking with her ballet teacher. On her D2W Roadmap, the lesson 'Three Questions for a Successful Journey' is mapped out on the road. Her answers to the three pertinent questions is the path she will follow to be successful toward her DREAM Cloud. Her answers demonstrate that she is aware of her current accomplishments toward her DREAM Cloud, the next actions that will lead her to the finish line, and what additional supports she will need to be successful.

Now, you have seen Janice's D2W Roadmap, find the blank D2W Roadmap. It is time for you to create your own D2W Roadmap. You can create one for each of your DREAM Clouds. Your Dream Cloud is at the top of the page. The four D2W life management tools are graphically portrayed in the car diagram. You should see the windshield, the hood, the steering wheel, the gearshift, and the control panel gauges. If you review your 'D2W: It's Your Turn' sections, you can use some of your answers to fill in the D2W Roadmap.

Step 1: WINDSHIELD: What do you see for your life? What do you see outside of the windshield? What do you want to accomplish in the next 6 months, 1 year, 3 , 5, or 10 years? This is a life-affirming vision statement you can speak daily about your life. Write "I see myself (fill in the blank)."

Step 2: Fill in one of your DREAM Clouds. (Lesson 1) Answer the question: What do I want to BE, HAVE, or EXPERIENCE?

Step 3: Choose a few descriptive words for your VIPC profile. Review the 20 D-R-E-A-M character keys. (Lesson 6 and Lesson 10) Choose five character keys you will demonstrate to "unlock" your DREAM Cloud.

Step 4: Write out your six S-M-A-R-T steering wheel goals related to your DREAM Cloud or your life in general. (Lesson 11)

Step 5: Write a few decisions and actions you have made or will make related to your DREAM Cloud. (Lesson 12 and Lesson 14)

Step 6: Referencing the five control gauges, list any problems you are facing or might face in accomplishing your DREAM Cloud. Evaluate your current performance in the five areas. (Lesson 18)

Post your D2W Roadmap somewhere you can view daily on your wall in your room. Make a copy and place it in your notebook. It is now time for action. Do the work it takes to make your dreams a reality. Evaluate your plan daily or weekly and mark your performance with a star for your accomplishments. The D2W Roadmap is used with your D2W Steering

Wheel Action plan, which is list all the goals and actions for your dream clouds. If you have demonstrated a character key you have targeted, circle the word and put a star by the character key. Write a descriptive sentence on what you did to demonstrate that character key. If you have accomplished the goals you wrote down, color the appropriate circle and mark with a star. When you have made good decisions, place a checkmark by the appropriate gear and briefly write out your major decisions. When you have solved a problem represented by the five control gauges, write a number to rate how well you are progressing in the 5 areas. Write out the problems encountered and what actions you took to solve them.

Your D2W Roadmap should be filled with stars, checkmarks, or whatever symbols you choose to reflect your accomplishments. When you have succeeded at your DREAM Cloud, color it in and place the date you accomplished your dream. If you are still pursuing your DREAM Cloud, mark the dates when you have achieved important milestones that move you closer to the finish line. Write what you are learning about yourself from the D2W lessons on the road. Use the D2W Roadmap to stay focused. **Celebrate your progress. Drive your life to its highest destinations.** Go and live your greatest possible life. You have what you need to win. You have the D2W Life Management System to use for the rest of your life. Believe me, you will need it no matter what age you are. **Show others how to win.** Show them what D2W is all about. Show them the system. **Be Driven 2 Win. Be D2W. See you on the road.**

Bringing D2W to Your Community

DREAMbuilders Youth Mentoring Network organization (DREAMbuilders) wants to partner with your school, community organization, or faith-based organization. It would be my pleasure to come and speak personally at a school graduation, school rally, or a special youth event. As a complement to the *'Are You Driven 2 Win: A Roadmap for Young People to Succeed in Life'* inspirational activity workbook, DREAMbuilders would like to introduce the online, e-learning Driven 2 Win: Personal Development and Youth Leadership curriculum to the young people in your organization. Additionally, the DREAMbuilders' DREAMStar youth performance and leadership team would love to come to your community and conduct a Driven 2 Win: Student Success Seminar or workshop. Your school location or community could also be a site for our next D2W YouTube video shows. Let us come and film an episode of the Driven 2 Win: High School Experiment video show at your next youth rally, school presentation, or church youth event.

It is time for youth to be inspired to dream and plan their life's greatest aspirations.

Anything is possible when we…

SEE IT. BELIEVE IT. SPEAK IT. BE IT.

The only thing left is to **RECEIVE IT.**

DREAMS DO COME TRUE.

"UNLOCK the DREAM — IGNITE the PASSION."

SEE YOU ON THE ROAD.

Ramona S. Jones,

Founder and President of DREAMbuilders Youth Mentoring Network

Contact us and buy books at www.DREAMbuilders4life.org

FACEBOOK: DREAMbuilders Youth Mentoring Network

Instagram: DREAMbuilders4life

A Tribute to the Artist – Joaquin Junco Jr.

Joaquin Junco Jr. (Junco Canché) is a freelance cartoonist and graphic designer studying in Southern California for his BA in graphic design. He got his start in an underground zine in 2009.

Since then he has drawn for La Prensa News, the Southwestern College Sun, and the Cal State San Bernardino newspaper. His work has been exhibited in the Centro Cultural de la Raza (San Diego), the RAFFMA (San Bernardino) and the Watts Towers Arts Center (Los Angeles). He has received awards from the Journalism Association of Community Colleges, the San Diego Society of Professional Journalists, and the San Diego Press Club.

Contact Joaquin Junco Jr. at:

juncocanche@gmail.com

Instagram.com/juncocanche

Twitter.com/juncocanche

Acknowledgments

In the course of anyone's journey, there are always people to recognize for their continued support and willingness to share their gifts. Sometimes people do not read this section, but if you do, you will find several people on my long and winding road and how they were 'sent' to inform, guide, and warn me. I needed them and still need them. My journey has not been easy. In fact, it has been difficult to be D2W and remain faithful and believe until fear and doubt was stomped out. I thank all of my "mentors" who have spoken in my life and activated and agitated my mind and spirit to become uncomfortable with mediocrity.

I want to thank my incredible mother, Raydonna Sheryl Adams, for being an excellent example I still aspire to replicate. What an example to follow. Talk about best practices. It is your consistent presence and strength that has helped me as I endured the many valleys and mountains to harness my vision and humanity. Thank you for your prayers and belief that I was more than the sum of my failures.

To my Dad, who taught me that my Father is in Heaven - Thank you for showing me how Grace and Love conquers all. "All things work out for good to those who are called according to His purpose." Covenant relationships last a lifetime. I am glad I am connected to you, and you are my Dad.

To my loving, supportive, life partner and husband - Michael R. Jones. I know you love me deeply. I met you when the dream had resurfaced again. Thank you for allowing me to dig it up and breathe life into it again. You helped me limp along the road of faith with only a hope and a dream. You helped me to believe that the "substance of my faith" is worth holding on to. At least we have each other....

To my children's dad, William Joseph Berry - The most respectful and most committed dad. Here are your roses now. I humbly recognize you for sharing the vision with me at the beginning and cared about it as much as I did. You are a DREAMbuilder for life. Thank you for the undergirding of our daughters.

To all my pastors who spoke God's words into me and encouraged me along the way - Pastor E. Wayne Gaddis Sr., Pastor Thomas Davis, Pastor Carolyn Riggins, Pastor Ray Kirkland, Pastor Al Furey, Pastor Frank and Jan Harper, Pastor Gary Phillips, Bishop Dixon, Bishop McKinney, Pastor Reginald Gary – Thank you for your patience and prayers. I love you all and thank you for every word you have spoken over my life. I bless you with all that is within me. I love you for being everything God called you to be. You have mentored me for decades, and I am because you are.

To my lifelong friend, John Weber - You are forever imprinted on my heart and soul. You challenge me to be my best and you inspire me to drive to my highest destinations. Our trophies are in heaven. I am sure there is a speech coach waiting to give us trophies even up there. ☺

To my trusted work colleague and Dynamic Duo, Wilfredo Perez - Thank you for being my first book editor and inspiring me to keep going with the book. Thanks for being a soundboard for someone who could not be boxed up and needed desperately to "get off the plantation." Someone had to be a runner; it had to be me. That's my next book. ☺

Lakeysha Sowunmi - Thank you for speaking the word over me to "resurrect" the dream when it was buried. "Your gift will make room for you and bring you before kings and queens."

To my literary geniuses - Judith Cochran, your expertise to get DREAMbuilders on the written page through press releases and guidance is much appreciated. Linda Berry, thank you for your educational consultation throughout this effort. Kay Collier, You have a place in my heart forever. Thank you for your eagle eye for review and your belief in the gift. You saw beyond the humanity to the eternal. I appreciate you for that. Erica Salcuni, you are brilliant, fun, and a talented writer. Thank you for letting me speak when I was still convincing myself. Stay connected to your passion and gift. You are loved. Nekose Wills, thank you for being a thorough editor and a 'thorn' to provide enough agitation until I surrendered. The next book should not be so difficult to edit. Demetrius Bedgood, thank you for modeling your gift of poetic prose to help guide me. Thanks Ryan from Smooth Writing for final editing.

Thank you Mykeah Simpson for your frontrunner example and inspiring me to finish what I started by completing your written work.

God's angels - James Patton, Elder Powell, and Carolyn 'Coco' Hunt. Thank you for carrying me the last miles when I desperately needed people to hang on to. You were there. You are my lifetime friends and family. Galatians 6:2 "Bear one another's burdens." You did that for me when I was crippled and I was on the side of the road with my vision. Thank you from the depths of my soul. You revived me with the life that was in you. Eternal blessings for working the magic of your gifts.

I wanted to make sure I gave a special place of appreciation for my cartoon illustrationist Joaquin Junco Jr. who created the D2W characters. Thanks for seeing the vision and for your patience on this journey. Young people will never be the same again once the D2W characters and brand take root in their hearts and minds of what it truly means to be D2W. Your gift will bless them as they journey toward their dreams.

To every young person who allowed me the honor to speak and share DREAMbuilders with them. With every fiber of my being I call forth your greatness to take its place of honor. You can; You will. Your greatness starts within. Never despise the power of the seed. Everything begins with the seed of your dream. Don't let the small things around you snuff out the fire that burns within. (Big Thanks to DREAMStar actors and crew: Issac, Rose, Stefani, Alexis, Sha'Miracle, Tyleriah, Christian, Johnny, Da'John, Angel, Laterra, Deleon, Kayla, Joshua, Sarai, Rile, Ty, and more ---- you paved the way for others to be DREAMbuilders. Thank you.)

To all the future DREAMbuilders who sense destiny calling them toward a great future: Please do not give up. Please do not shrink down or lessen your grip on your future. Discover your calling. Let FAITH take you to the place of your destiny. Take hold. Take courage. Keep pushing forward. Dreams do come true. See it. Believe it. Speak it. Be it. Receive it. Ask, Seek, Knock. Doors are opening for you right now.

APPENDICES

D2W Roadmaps – D2W Characters

D2W Roadmap – Blank

D2W Steering Wheel Action Plans – D2W Characters

D2W Steering Wheel Action Plan – Blank

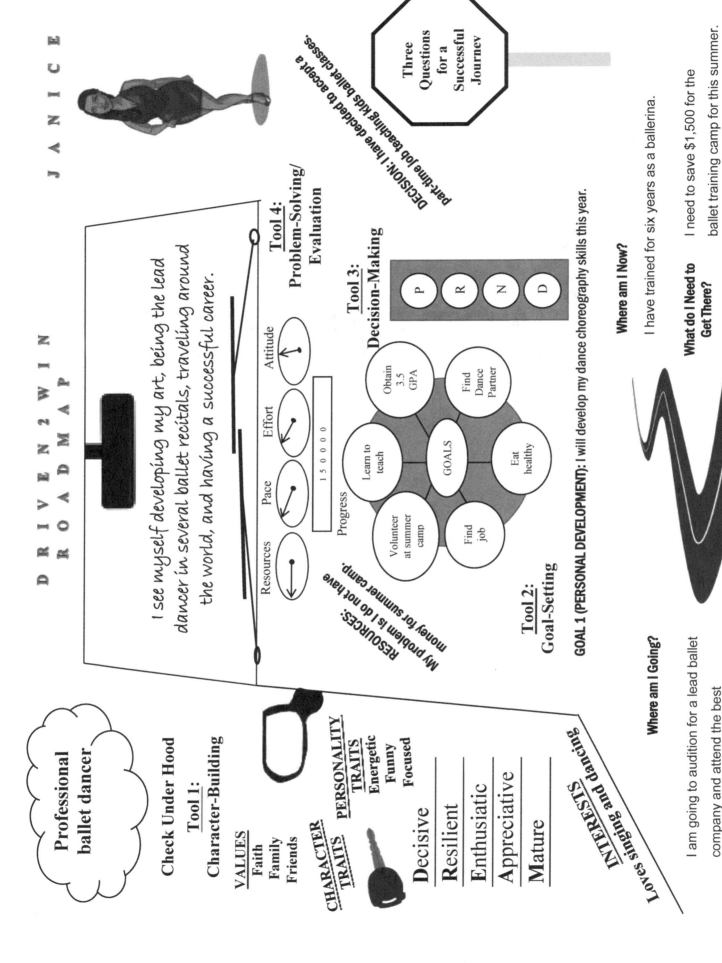

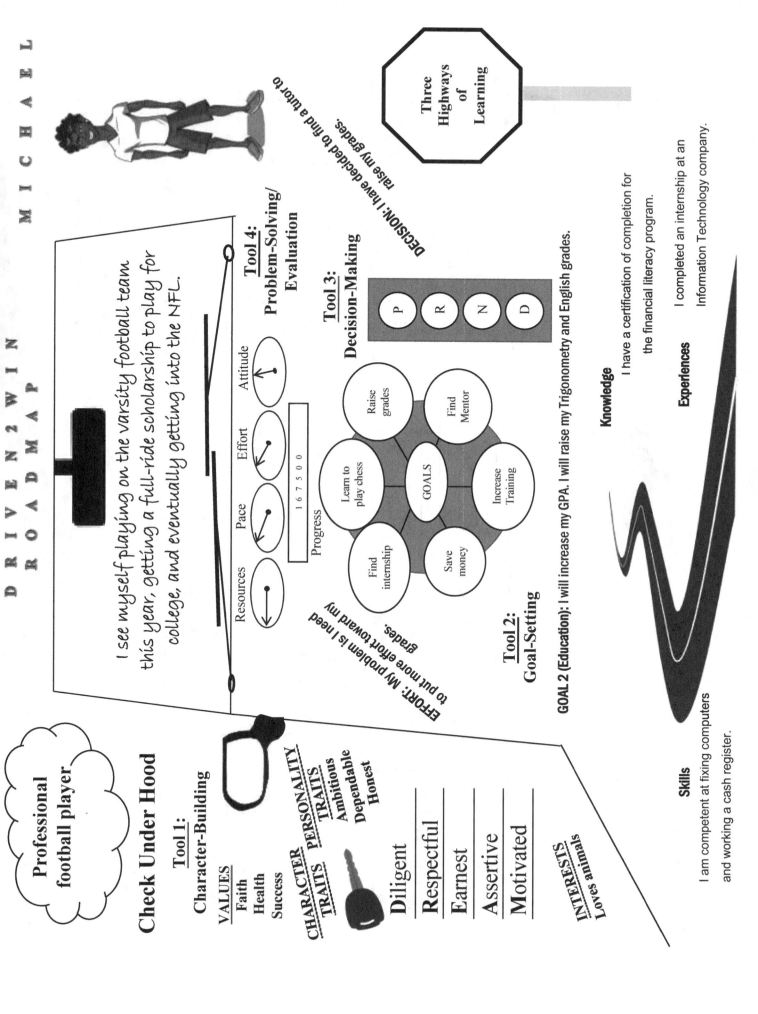

MICHAEL

DRIVEN2WIN ROADMAP

Professional football player

I see myself playing on the varsity football team this year, getting a full-ride scholarship to play for college, and eventually getting into the NFL.

Check Under Hood

Tool 1: Character-Building

VALUES
Faith
Health
Success

CHARACTER TRAITS
Diligent
Respectful
Earnest
Assertive
Motivated

PERSONALITY TRAITS
Ambitious
Dependable
Honest

INTERESTS
Loves animals

Tool 4: Problem-Solving/Evaluation

DECISION: I have decided to find a tutor to raise my grades.

Resources   Pace   Effort   Attitude

Progress   1 6 7 5 0 0

EFFORT: My problem is I need to put more effort toward my grades.

Tool 3: Decision-Making

P   R   N   D

Tool 2: Goal-Setting

GOALS
Raise grades
Find Mentor
Increase Training
Save money
Find internship
Learn to play chess

GOAL 2 (Education): I will increase my GPA. I will raise my Trigonometry and English grades.

Three Highways of Learning

Knowledge
I have a certification of completion for the financial literacy program.

Experiences
I completed an internship at an Information Technology company.

Skills
I am competent at fixing computers and working a cash register.

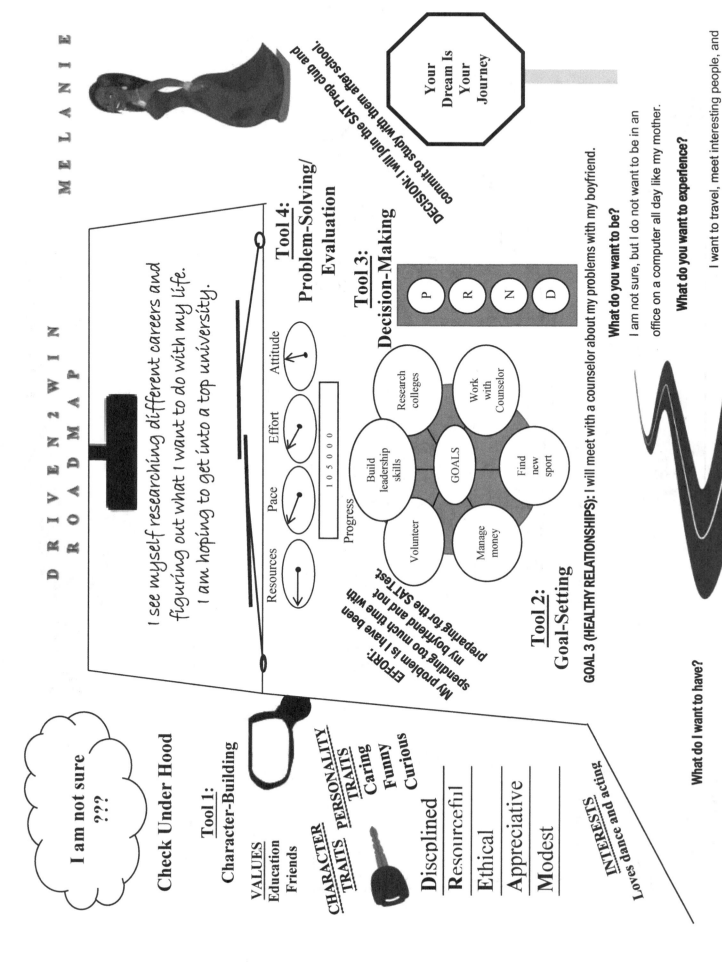

MELANIE

DRIVEN2WIN
ROADMAP

I see myself researching different careers and figuring out what I want to do with my life. I am hoping to get into a top university.

Your Dream Is Your Journey

Tool 4: Problem-Solving/ Evaluation

DECISION: I will join the SAT prep club and commit to study with them after school.

Tool 3: Decision-Making

P R N D

Progress

Resources Pace Effort Attitude

1 0 5 0 0 0

GOAL 3 (HEALTHY RELATIONSHIPS): I will meet with a counselor about my problems with my boyfriend.

What do you want to be?
I am not sure, but I do not want to be in an office on a computer all day like my mother.

What do you want to experience?
I want to travel, meet interesting people, and help needy children.

Tool 2: Goal-Setting

Research colleges
Work with Counselor
Build leadership skills
GOALS
Find new sport
Volunteer
Manage money

EFFORT: My problem is I have been spending too much time with my boyfriend and not preparing for the SAT Test.

What do I want to have?
I want to have a life where I am creative and outgoing.

I am not sure ???

Check Under Hood

Tool 1: Character-Building

VALUES
Education
Friends

CHARACTER TRAITS
Disciplined
Resourceful
Ethical
Appreciative
Modest

PERSONALITY TRAITS
Caring
Funny
Curious

INTERESTS
Loves dance and acting

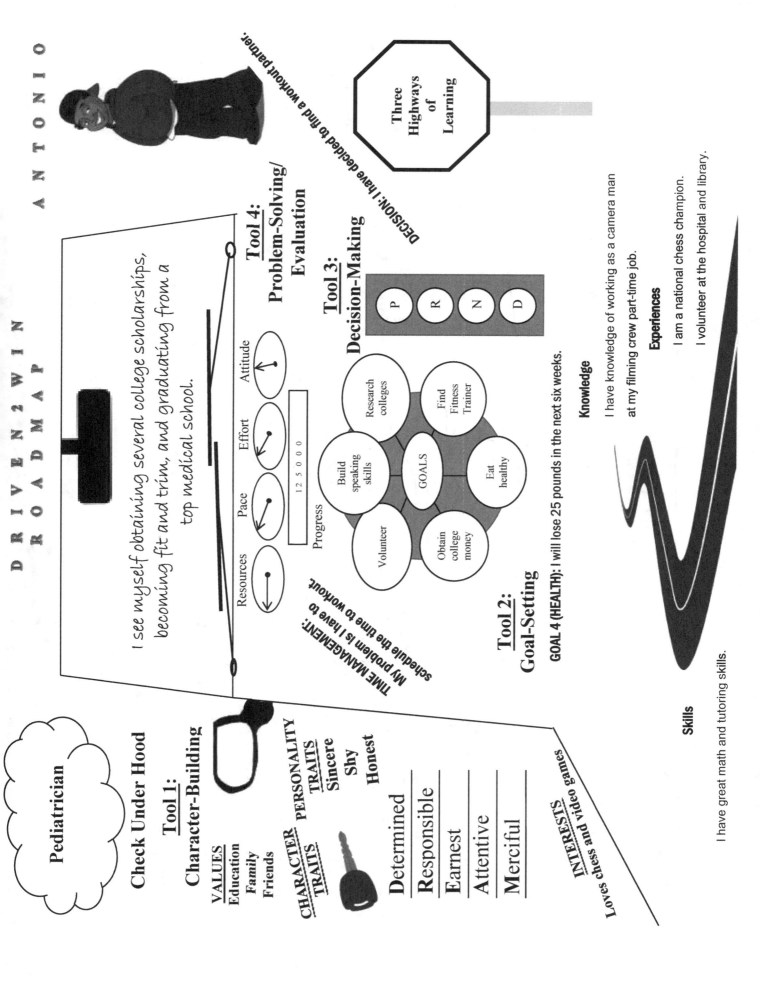

ANTONIO

DRIVEN2WIN ROADMAP

Pediatrician

I see myself obtaining several college scholarships, becoming fit and trim, and graduating from a top medical school.

Check Under Hood

Tool 1: Character-Building

VALUES
Education
Family
Friends

CHARACTER TRAITS

PERSONALITY TRAITS
Sincere
Shy
Honest

Determined
Responsible
Earnest
Attentive
Merciful

INTERESTS
Loves chess and video games

TIME MANAGEMENT:
My problem is I have to schedule the time to workout.

Resources   Pace   Effort   Attitude

Progress   1 2 5 0 0 0

Tool 4: Problem-Solving/Evaluation

Tool 3: Decision-Making

P
R
N
D

Research colleges
Find Fitness Trainer
Build speaking skills
GOALS
Eat healthy
Volunteer
Obtain college money

Tool 2: Goal-Setting

GOAL 4 (HEALTH): I will lose 25 pounds in the next six weeks.

DECISION: I have decided to find a workout partner.

Three Highways of Learning

Knowledge

I have knowledge of working as a camera man

at my filming crew part-time job.

Experiences

I am a national chess champion.

I volunteer at the hospital and library.

Skills

I have great math and tutoring skills.

GREG

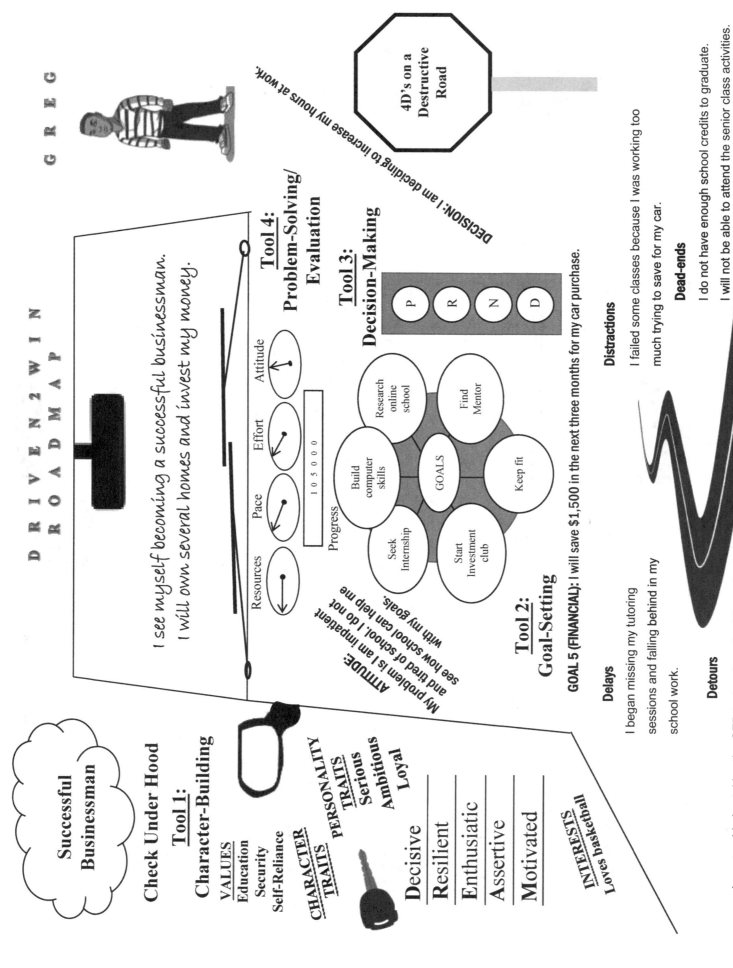

DRIVEN2WIN ROADMAP

I see myself becoming a successful businessman. I will own several homes and invest my money.

4D's on a Destructive Road

DECISION: I am deciding to increase my hours at work.

Tool 4: Problem-Solving/ Evaluation

Tool 3: Decision-Making

P R N D

Resources | Pace | Effort | Attitude

Progress 1 0 5 0 0 0

ATTITUDE: My problem is I am impatient and tired of school. I do not see how school can help me with my goals.

Tool 2: Goal-Setting

Research online school
Find Mentor
Build computer skills
GOALS
Keep fit
Seek Internship
Start Investment club

GOAL 5 (FINANCIAL): I will save $1,500 in the next three months for my car purchase.

Distractions
I failed some classes because I was working too much trying to save for my car.

Dead-ends
I do not have enough school credits to graduate.
I will not be able to attend the senior class activities.

Delays
I began missing my tutoring sessions and falling behind in my school work.

Detours
I am considering taking the GED test early and quitting school.

Successful Businessman

Check Under Hood

Tool 1: Character-Building

VALUES
Education
Security
Self-Reliance

CHARACTER TRAITS

PERSONALITY TRAITS
Serious
Ambitious
Loyal

Decisive
Resilient
Enthusiatic
Assertive
Motivated

INTERESTS
Loves basketball

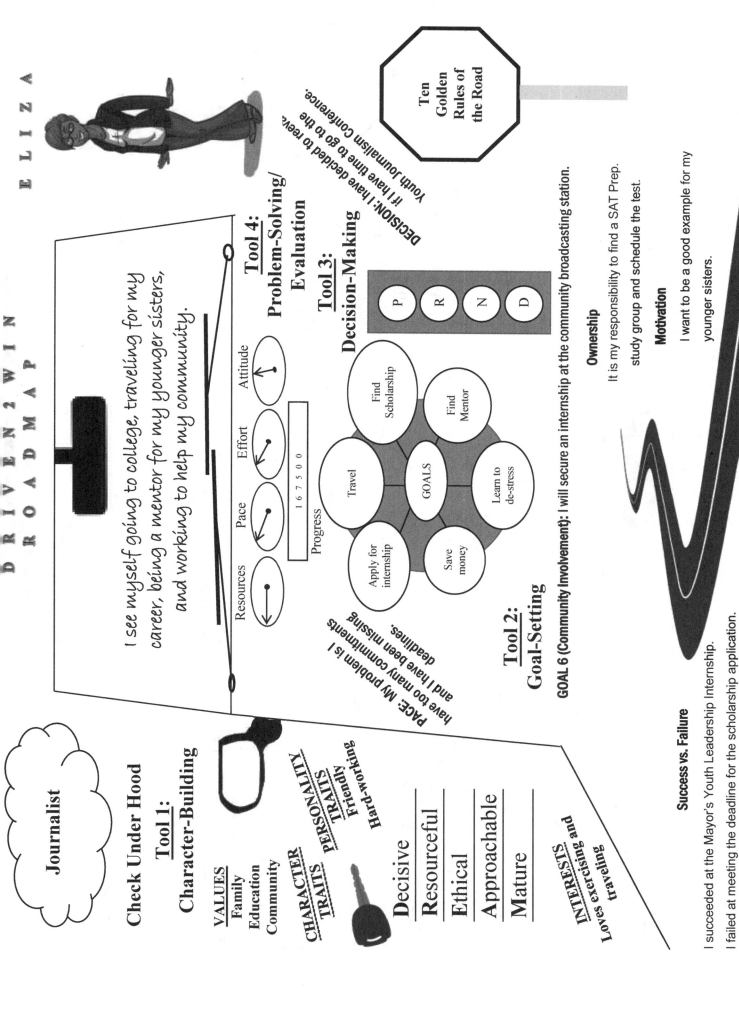

ELIZA

DRIVEN2WIN ROADMAP

Journalist

I see myself going to college, traveling for my career, being a mentor for my younger sisters, and working to help my community.

Check Under Hood

Tool 1: Character-Building

VALUES
Family
Education
Community

CHARACTER TRAITS

PERSONALITY TRAITS
Friendly
Hard-working

Decisive
Resourceful
Ethical
Approachable
Mature

INTERESTS
Loves exercising and traveling

Resources   Pace   Effort   Attitude

Progress   1 6 7 5 0 0

Tool 4: Problem-Solving/ Evaluation

Tool 3: Decision-Making

DECISION: I have decided to reeve. if I have time to go to the Youth Journalism Conference.

PACE: My problem is I have too many commitments and I have been missing deadlines.

Ten Golden Rules of the Road

P R N D

GOALS
Find Scholarship
Find Mentor
Travel
Learn to de-stress
Apply for internship
Save money

Tool 2: Goal-Setting

GOAL 6 (Community Involvement): I will secure an internship at the community broadcasting station.

Ownership
It is my responsibility to find a SAT Prep. study group and schedule the test.

Motivation
I want to be a good example for my younger sisters.

Success vs. Failure

I succeeded at the Mayor's Youth Leadership Internship.

I failed at meeting the deadline for the scholarship application.

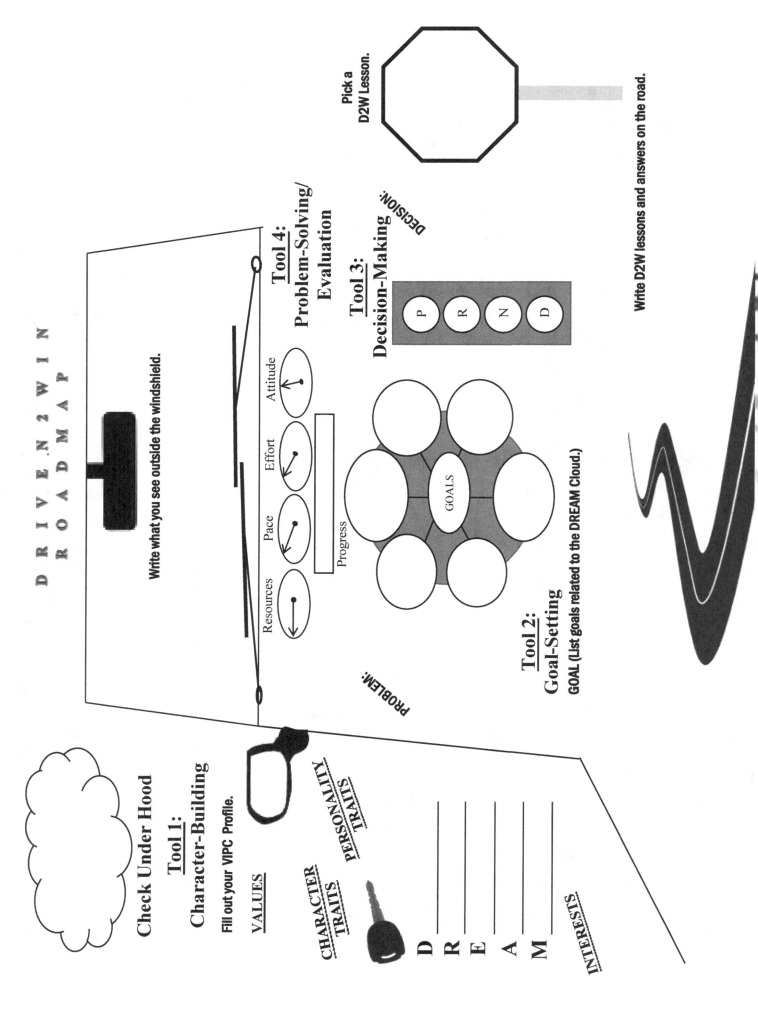

D R I V E N . 2 . W I N
R O A D M A P

Write what you see outside the windshield.

Tool 4:
Problem-Solving/
Evaluation

Resources | Pace | Effort | Attitude

Progress

DECISION:

Tool 3:
Decision-Making

P R N D

PROBLEM:

GOALS

Tool 2:
Goal-Setting

GOAL (List goals related to the DREAM Cloud.)

Pick a
D2W Lesson.

Write D2W lessons and answers on the road.

Check Under Hood

Tool 1:
Character-Building

Fill out your VIPC Profile.

VALUES

CHARACTER
TRAITS

PERSONALITY
TRAITS

D _____
R _____
E _____
A _____
M _____

INTERESTS

Driven 2 Win Steering Wheel Action Plan

Today's Date: _____

(Evaluation Period: October 1 – December 30)

GOAL 1: PERSONAL DEVELOPMENT	Resources	Time Mgt	Effort	Attitude	Progress
	3	4	5	3	3
Action 1: *Sign up for ballet dance choreography classes on the weekend.*	X	Due Date		Completed Date	
		Oct 10		Oct 22	
Action 2: *Join the ASB school club and work on school fundraising campaigns.*	X	Due Date		Completed Date	
		Oct 22		Oct 18	
Action 3: *Complete the 20-hour Driven 2 Win Youth Leadership Program.*	X	Due Date		Completed Date	
		Nov 15		Nov 15	
GOAL 2: EDUCATION (Higher Learning)	Resources	Time Mgt	Effort	Attitude	Progress
	3	4	5	3	3
Action 1: *Increase grade point average from 3.2 gpa to 3.5 gpa.*	X	Due Date		Completed Date	
		Nov 20		Nov 20	
Action 2: *Enroll and complete the 6-week SAT Prep. workshops.*		Due Date		Completed Date	
		Dec 10		*In progress*	
Action 3: *Work with a tutor and raise Chemistry grade to 90% grade or higher.*		Due Date		Completed Date	
		Dec 15		*In progress*	
GOAL 3: HEALTHY RELATIONSHIPS	Resources	Time Mgt	Effort	Attitude	Progress
	3	4	5	3	3
Action 1: *Send thank you cards to three relatives for school donations.*	X	Due Date		Completed Date	
		Oct 15		Oct 20	
Action 2: *Find new ballet instructor for upcoming ballet competition by November.*	X	Due Date		Completed Date	
		Oct 22		Oct 15	
Action 3: *Meet with D2W Leadership team and career mentor two times per month.*		Due Date		Completed Date	
		Nov 30		*In progress*	
GOAL 4: HEALTH, NUTRITION, & FITNESS	Resources	Time Mgt	Effort	Attitude	Progress
	3	4	3	3	3
Action 1: *Find workout partner and trainer and workout for 1 hour 4 days per week.*	X	Due Date		Completed Date	
		Nov 20		Nov 20	
Action 2: *Eat at least 4 to 5 servings of fruits and vegetables daily for six weeks.*		Due Date		Completed Date	
		Nov 30		*In progress*	
Action 3: *Attend the free yoga classes with mom to de-stress weekly.*	*N/A*	Due Date		Completed Date	
		Nov 30		*Didn't start*	
GOAL 5: FINANCIAL EDUCATION AND RESPONSIBILITY	Resources	Time Mgt	Effort	Attitude	Progress
	4	4	5	4	4
Action 1: *Open bank account and establish credit through credit card.*	X	Due Date		Completed Date	
		Oct 30		Oct 27	
Action 2: *Attend 6-week financial literacy boot camp for students.*	X	Due Date		Completed Date	
		Nov 30		Nov 19	
Action 3: *Save up $300 from babysitting job for ballet summer camp.*	X	Due Date		Completed Date	
		Oct 30		Nov 5	
GOAL 6: COMMUNITY INVOLVEMENT	Resources	Time Mgt	Effort	Attitude	Progress
	3	4	5	5	5
Action 1: *Research three community organizations for summer internships.*	X	Due Date		Completed Date	
		Nov 15		Nov 20	
Action 2: *Complete 10 hours of volunteer time in the next 3 months.*	X	Due Date		Completed Date	
		Nov 30		Oct 15	
Action 3: *Raise $1,500 for community kid ballet production with project team.*		Due Date		Completed Date	
		Dec 30		*In progress*	

Driven 2 Win Steering Wheel Action Plan

Today's Date: _____   (Evaluation Period: October 1 – December 30)

GOAL 1: PERSONAL DEVELOPMENT	Resources	Time Mgt	Effort	Attitude	Progress
	3	4	5	3	3
Action 1: *Read 'Teens can Make it Happen' book by Stedman Graham.*	X	Due Date: Oct 10		Completed Date: Oct 22	
Action 2: *Try out for Varsity football team and secure front-line position.*	X	Due Date: Oct 22		Completed Date: Oct 18	
Action 3: *Complete the 20-hour Driven 2 Win Youth Leadership Program.*	X	Due Date: Nov 15		Completed Date: Nov 15	

GOAL 2: EDUCATION (Higher Learning)	Resources	Time Mgt	Effort	Attitude	Progress
	4	3	3	3	3
Action 1: *Increase grade point average from 3.0 gpa to 3.5 gpa.*	X	Due Date: Nov 20		Completed Date: Nov 20	
Action 2: *Find a tutor for English and Trigonometry classes to raise test scores to 85% average or higher.*		Due Date: Dec 10		Completed Date: *In progress*	
Action 3: *Complete D2W Information Technology career industry research project.*		Due Date: Dec 15		Completed Date: *In progress*	

GOAL 3: HEALTHY RELATIONSHIPS	Resources	Time Mgt	Effort	Attitude	Progress
	4	4	5	4	4
Action 1: *Meet 5 potential career/business mentors and interview.*	X	Due Date: Oct 15		Completed Date: Oct 20	
Action 2: *Meet with career counselor and discuss school and career opportunities.*	X	Due Date: Oct 22		Completed Date: Oct 15	
Action 3: *Meet with D2W Leadership team and career mentor two times per month.*		Due Date: Nov 30		Completed Date: *In progress*	

GOAL 4: HEALTH, NUTRITION, & FITNESS	Resources	Time Mgt	Effort	Attitude	Progress
	5	4	5	5	4
Action 1: *Begin 8-week weight training program with new football conditioning trainer.*	X	Due Date: Oct 1		Completed Date: Nov 20	
Action 2: *Increase caloric intake to 3,000 calories to increase 10lbs.*	X	Due Date: Nov 15		Completed Date: Nov 25	
Action 3: *Setup and attend a minimum of 3 appointments with counselor to learn strategies on dealing with stress and depression.*	X	Due Date: Nov 15		Completed Date: Nov 5	

GOAL 5: FINANCIAL EDUCATION AND RESPONSIBILITY	Resources	Time Mgt	Effort	Attitude	Progress
	5	4	5	4	4
Action 1: *Prepare resume, practice interview questions, and find a part-time job.*	X	Due Date: Oct 30		Completed Date: Oct 27	
Action 2: *Attend 6-week financial literacy boot camp for students.*	X	Due Date: Nov 30		Completed Date: Nov 19	
Action 3: *Save up $500 for football skill-development training camp.*		Due Date: Oct 30		Completed Date: *In progress*	

GOAL 6: COMMUNITY INVOLVEMENT	Resources	Time Mgt	Effort	Attitude	Progress
	3	3	3	4	4
Action 1: *Participate in neighborhood clean-up project.*	X	Due Date: Oct 15		Completed Date: Oct 15	
Action 2: *Complete 10 hours of volunteer time in the next 3 months.*		Due Date: Oct 30		Completed Date: *In progress*	
Action 3: *Attend Young Men's Leadership and Empowerment Conference.*	X	Due Date: Nov 10		Completed Date: Nov 10	

Driven 2 Win Steering Wheel Action Plan

Today's Date: _____   (Evaluation Period: October 1 – December 30)

GOAL 1: PERSONAL DEVELOPMENT	Resources	Time Mgt	Effort	Attitude	Progress
	3	4	5	3	3
Action 1: *Submit poetry for online blog for young creative writers.*	X	Due Date		Completed Date	
		Oct 10		Oct 22	
Action 2: *Prepare routine for the cheerleading team captain tryouts.*	X	Due Date		Completed Date	
		Oct 22		Oct 18	
Action 3: *Learn Spanish and travel to Spain for a two-week Spring break vacation.*	X	Due Date		Completed Date	
		Nov 15		Nov 15	

GOAL 2: EDUCATION (Higher Learning)	Resources	Time Mgt	Effort	Attitude	Progress
	3	4	3	3	3
Action 1: *Increase grade point average from 3.5 gpa to 3.8 gpa.*	X	Due Date		Completed Date	
		Nov 20		Nov 20	
Action 2: *Enroll and complete the 6-week SAT Prep. workshops.*		Due Date		Completed Date	
		Dec 10		*In progress*	
Action 3: *Work with a tutor and raise Algebra grade to 85% grade or higher.*		Due Date		Completed Date	
		Dec 15		*In progress*	

GOAL 3: HEALTHY RELATIONSHIPS	Resources	Time Mgt	Effort	Attitude	Progress
	3	4	5	3	4
Action 1: *Make appointment with school psychologist on issues dealing with dating and depression.*	X	Due Date		Completed Date	
		Oct 15		Oct 20	
Action 2: *Participate in church youth group weekly as a youth leader for middle school group on weekends.*	X	Due Date		Completed Date	
		Oct 30		Oct 30	
Action 3: *Meet with D2W Leadership team and career mentor two times per month.*		Due Date		Completed Date	
		Nov 30		*In progress*	

GOAL 4: HEALTH, NUTRITION, & FITNESS	Resources	Time Mgt	Effort	Attitude	Progress
	3	3	3	3	3
Action 1: *Start working out with cheerleading squad two times per week.*	X	Due Date		Completed Date	
		Oct 30		Oct 25	
Action 2: *Eat at least 4 to 5 servings of fruits and vegetables daily for six weeks.*	X	Due Date		Completed Date	
		Nov 15		Nov 15	
Action 3: *Attend five-session community nutrition classes.*		Due Date		Completed Date	
		Nov 30		*Did not complete*	

GOAL 5: FINANCIAL EDUCATION AND RESPONSIBILITY	Resources	Time Mgt	Effort	Attitude	Progress
	4	4	5	4	4
Action 1: *Read 'Rich Dad, Poor Dad' book by Roberty Kiyosaki on financial literacy.*	X	Due Date		Completed Date	
		Oct 30		Oct 30	
Action 2: *Attend 6-week financial literacy boot camp for students.*	X	Due Date		Completed Date	
		Nov 30		Nov 19	
Action 3: *Save $800 for Spring vacation trip.*	X	Due Date		Completed Date	
		Oct 30		Oct 15	

GOAL 6: COMMUNITY INVOLVEMENT	Resources	Time Mgt	Effort	Attitude	Progress
	4	4	5	5	5
Action 1: *Become a member of the DREAMbuilders Youth Mentoring Network organization.*	X	Due Date		Completed Date	
		Oct 10		Oct 5	
Action 2: *Complete 10 hours of volunteer time in the next 3 months.*	X	Due Date		Completed Date	
		Nov 30		Nov 25	
Action 3: *Organize and participate in the Homeless Ministry team event.*	X	Due Date		Completed Date	
		Nov 22		Nov 22	

Driven 2 Win Steering Wheel Action Plan

Today's Date: _____   (Evaluation Period: October 1 – December 30)

GOAL 1: PERSONAL DEVELOPMENT	Resources	Time Mgt	Effort	Attitude	Progress
	5	4	5	4	4
Action 1: *Run for President of the Chess school club.*	X	Due Date		Completed Date	
		Oct 10		Oct 10	
Action 2: *Read '7 Habits of Highly Effective Teens' by Sean Covey*	X	Due Date		Completed Date	
		Oct 22		Oct 16	
Action 3: *Complete the 20-hour Driven 2 Win Youth Leadership Program.*	X	Due Date		Completed Date	
		Nov 15		Nov 15	

GOAL 2: EDUCATION (Higher Learning)	Resources	Time Mgt	Effort	Attitude	Progress
	5	4	5	4	5
Action 1: *Research scholarships for medical school applications.*	X	Due Date		Completed Date	
		Nov 20		Nov 20	
Action 2: *Enroll and complete the 6-week SAT Prep. Workshops.*	☐	Due Date		Completed Date	
		Dec 10		*In progress*	
Action 3: *Maintain 4.0+ gpa average.*	☐	Due Date		Completed Date	
		Dec 15		*In progress*	

GOAL 3: HEALTHY RELATIONSHIPS	Resources	Time Mgt	Effort	Attitude	Progress
	3	4	5	5	4
Action 1: *Send thank you cards to mentors for Letters of Recommendations.*	X	Due Date		Completed Date	
		Oct 15		Oct 15	
Action 2: *Help younger brother prepare his resume and research part-time jobs.*	X	Due Date		Completed Date	
		Oct 30		Oct 29	
Action 3: *Meet with D2W Leadership team and career mentor two times per month.*	☐	Due Date		Completed Date	
		Nov 30		*In progress*	

GOAL 4: HEALTH, NUTRITION, & FITNESS	Resources	Time Mgt	Effort	Attitude	Progress
	4	4	3	3	3
Action 1: *Find workout trainer and train three times per week for 1 hour.*	☐	Due Date		Completed Date	
		Dec 30		*In progress*	
Action 2: *Eat at least 4 to 5 servings of fruits and vegetables daily for six each month.*	X	Due Date		Completed Date	
		Nov 30		Nov 30	
Action 3: *Attend five-session community nutrition classes.*	X	Due Date		Completed Date	
		Oct 30		Oct 25	

GOAL 5: FINANCIAL EDUCATION AND RESPONSIBILITY	Resources	Time Mgt	Effort	Attitude	Progress
	4	4	5	4	4
Action 1: *Start tutoring business and work with 5 to 10 students per month.*	X	Due Date		Completed Date	
		Oct 30		Oct 27	
Action 2: *Save $1,000 to buy tickets to Comic Com event next summer.*	☐	Due Date		Completed Date	
		Dec 30		*In progress*	
Action 3: *Attend 6-week financial literacy boot camp for students.*	X	Due Date		Completed Date	
		Nov 30		Nov 30	

GOAL 6: COMMUNITY INVOLVEMENT	Resources	Time Mgt	Effort	Attitude	Progress
	4	4	5	5	5
Action 1: *Sign up and participate in walk/run for Diabetes research.*	X	Due Date		Completed Date	
		Oct 20		Oct 20	
Action 2: *Complete 10 hours of volunteer time in the next 3 months.*	X	Due Date		Completed Date	
		Nov 30		Nov 25	
Action 3: *Raise $800 for D2W Youth Leadership Team.*	☐	Due Date		Completed Date	
		Dec 30		*In progress*	

Driven 2 Win Steering Wheel Action Plan

Today's Date: _____   (Evaluation Period: October 1 – December 30)

GOAL 1: PERSONAL DEVELOPMENT

	Resources	Time Mgt	Effort	Attitude	Progress
	4	3	5	4	5

Action 1: *Read 'Life Strategies for Teens' by Jay McGraw.*	X	Due Date	Completed Date
		Oct 10	Oct 22

Action 2: *Take free 3-session computer classes at the Employment Development Department.*	X	Due Date	Completed Date
		Oct 22	Oct 18

Action 3: *Complete the 20-hour Driven 2 Win Youth Leadership Program.*	X	Due Date	Completed Date
		Nov 15	Nov 15

GOAL 2: EDUCATION (Higher Learning)

	Resources	Time Mgt	Effort	Attitude	Progress
	3	4	5	3	3

Action 1: *Increase grade point average from 2.5 gpa to 3.0 gpa.*		Due Date	Completed Date
		Nov 30	*In progress*

Action 2: *Make an appointment with school counselor to research and discuss online classes.*	X	Due Date	Completed Date
		Nov 30	Nov 15

Action 3: *Attend study group sessions to make up missing homework in English and Chemistry classes.*		Due Date	Completed Date
		Nov 30	*In progress*

GOAL 3: HEALTHY RELATIONSHIPS

	Resources	Time Mgt	Effort	Attitude	Progress
	3	4	5	3	3

Action 1: *Conduct personality test with friends as a D2W project.*	X	Due Date	Completed Date
		Oct 15	Oct 15

Action 2: *Get the business cards of 3 career professionals and 3 business professionals.*	X	Due Date	Completed Date
		Oct 22	Oct 22

Action 3: *Attend D2W career/business mentor meetups monthly.*		Due Date	Completed Date
		Nov 30	*In progress*

GOAL 4: HEALTH, NUTRITION, & FITNESS

	Resources	Time Mgt	Effort	Attitude	Progress
	3	4	3	3	3

Action 1: *Tryout for basketball team for starter position.*	X	Due Date	Completed Date
		Nov 20	Nov 20

Action 2: *Weight light 3 times per week with workout partner.*		Due Date	Completed Date
		Nov 30	*In progress*

Action 3: *Drink daily protein shake in the mornings before workouts.*		Due Date	Completed Date
		Dec 30	*In progress*

GOAL 5: FINANCIAL EDUCATION AND RESPONSIBILITY

	Resources	Time Mgt	Effort	Attitude	Progress
	4	4	5	4	4

Action 1: *Read 'Rich Dad, Poor Dad' book by Roberty Kiyosaki on financial literacy.*	X	Due Date	Completed Date
		Oct 30	Oct 27

Action 2: *Save $2,500 for car purchase.*	X	Due Date	Completed Date
		Nov 30	Nov 15

Action 3: *Attend the 12-week youth entrepreneurial program.*		Due Date	Completed Date
		Dec 30	*In progress*

GOAL 6: COMMUNITY INVOLVEMENT

	Resources	Time Mgt	Effort	Attitude	Progress
	3	4	4	5	5

Action 1: *Research three community organizations for summer internships.*	X	Due Date	Completed Date
		Nov 15	Nov 20

Action 2: *Complete 10 hours of volunteer time in the next 3 months.*	X	Due Date	Completed Date
		Nov 30	Oct 15

Action 3: *Raise $800 for D2W Youth Leadership Team.*		Due Date	Completed Date
		Dec 30	*In progress*

Driven 2 Win Steering Wheel Action Plan

Today's Date: _____   (Evaluation Period: October 1 – December 30)

GOAL 1: PERSONAL DEVELOPMENT	Resources	Time Mgt	Effort	Attitude	Progress
	3	4	5	3	3
Action 1: *Join the Yearbook school club as a reporter.*	X	Due Date		Completed Date	
		Sep 30		Sep 15	
Action 2: *Sign-up for the overseas missions trip to Europe.*	X	Due Date		Completed Date	
		Oct 30		Sep 30	
Action 3: *Complete the 20-hour Driven 2 Win Youth Leadership Program.*	X	Due Date		Completed Date	
		Nov 15		Nov 15	

GOAL 2: EDUCATION (Higher Learning)	Resources	Time Mgt	Effort	Attitude	Progress
	3	4	5	4	4
Action 1: *Increase grade point average from 3.7 gpa to 4.0 gpa.*	☐	Due Date		Completed Date	
		Nov 20		*In progress*	
Action 2: *Enroll and complete the 6-week SAT Prep. Workshops.*	☐	Due Date		Completed Date	
		Nov 30		*In progress*	
Action 3: *Work with study group weekly for AP homework and test preparation.*	☐	Due Date		Completed Date	
		Dec 30		*In progress*	

GOAL 3: HEALTHY RELATIONSHIPS	Resources	Time Mgt	Effort	Attitude	Progress
	3	4	5	3	3
Action 1: *Host international student at home for six weeks.*	X	Due Date		Completed Date	
		Oct 30		Oct 30	
Action 2: *Sign up to be a peer mentor in DREAMbuilders youth mentoring program.*	X	Due Date		Completed Date	
		Nov 30		Nov 15	
Action 3: *Meet with D2W Leadership team and career mentor two times per month.*	☐	Due Date		Completed Date	
		Nov 30		*In progress*	

GOAL 4: HEALTH, NUTRITION, & FITNESS	Resources	Time Mgt	Effort	Attitude	Progress
	3	4	3	3	3
Action 1: *Walk to distress after dinner with family at least 3 times per week.*	X	Due Date		Completed Date	
		Dec 30		*Ongoing*	
Action 2: *Eat breakfast daily and pack lunch for school.*	☐	Due Date		Completed Date	
		Dec 30		*Ongoing*	
Action 3: *Make monthly appointment to speak with counselor.*	X	Due Date		Completed Date	
		Nov 30		Nov 1	

GOAL 5: FINANCIAL EDUCATION AND RESPONSIBILITY	Resources	Time Mgt	Effort	Attitude	Progress
	4	4	5	4	4
Action 1: *Find part-time job.*	X	Due Date		Completed Date	
		Oct 30		Oct 25	
Action 2: *Attend 6-week financial literacy boot camp for students.*	X	Due Date		Completed Date	
		Nov 30		Nov 19	
Action 3: *Work on Youth Entrepreneur project to raise $1,500 for travel plans.*	X	Due Date		Completed Date	
		Oct 30		Nov 5	

GOAL 6: COMMUNITY INVOLVEMENT	Resources	Time Mgt	Effort	Attitude	Progress
	3	4	5	5	5
Action 1: *Submit application for Mayor's Youth Internship program.*	X	Due Date		Completed Date	
		Nov 15		Nov 20	
Action 2: *Complete 10 hours of volunteer time in the next 3 months.*	X	Due Date		Completed Date	
		Nov 30		Nov 15	
Action 3: *Organize Homeless Care neighborhood project and seek donations for personal care items.*	☐	Due Date		Completed Date	
		Dec 30		*In progress*	

Driven 2 Win Steering Wheel Action Plan

Today's Date: _____   (Evaluation Period: _____)

GOAL 1: PERSONAL DEVELOPMENT	Resources	Time Mgt	Effort	Attitude	Progress
Action 1:	☐	Due Date		Completed Date	
Action 2:	☐	Due Date		Completed Date	
Action 3:	☐	Due Date		Completed Date	

GOAL 2: EDUCATION (Higher Learning)	Resources	Time Mgt	Effort	Attitude	Progress
Action 1:	☐	Due Date		Completed Date	
Action 2:	☐	Due Date		Completed Date	
Action 3:	☐	Due Date		Completed Date	

GOAL 3: HEALTHY RELATIONSHIPS	Resources	Time Mgt	Effort	Attitude	Progress
Action 1:	☐	Due Date		Completed Date	
Action 2:	☐	Due Date		Completed Date	
Action 3:	☐	Due Date		Completed Date	

GOAL 4: HEALTH, NUTRITION, & FITNESS	Resources	Time Mgt	Effort	Attitude	Progress
Action 1:	☐	Due Date		Completed Date	
Action 2:	☐	Due Date		Completed Date	
Action 3:	☐	Due Date		Completed Date	

GOAL 5: FINANCIAL EDUCATION AND RESPONSIBILITY	Resources	Time Mgt	Effort	Attitude	Progress
Action 1:	☐	Due Date		Completed Date	
Action 2:	☐	Due Date		Completed Date	
Action 3:	☐	Due Date		Completed Date	

GOAL 6: COMMUNITY INVOLVEMENT	Resources	Time Mgt	Effort	Attitude	Progress
Action 1:	☐	Due Date		Completed Date	
Action 2:	☐	Due Date		Completed Date	
Action 3:	☐	Due Date		Completed Date	

About The Author

Ramona Jones is an inspirational speaker and the Founder and President of DREAMbuilders Youth Mentoring Network (DREAMbuilders), a member-based youth leadership and mentoring organization headquartered in San Diego, California. With the mission to inspire young people ages 12 – 21 to pursue and accomplish their dreams and goals, DREAMbuilders implements effective enrichment programs to educate, equip, and empower them to prepare for personal, academic, social, career, and entrepreneurial success. Ramona Jones holds a Bachelor's Degree in Business Administration and a Master's Degree in Management. "I believe young people need to qualify for promotion through their commitment to personal development as they discover their strengths and gifts to unleash their passion to live their fullest life. Every youth has a dream and a purpose. Every youth desires to unlock their dreams and experience personal satisfaction. As they discover who they are, develop a guiding vision, and do the hard work, they will uncover their greatness."